HELP! I'M AN URBAN YOUTH WORKER!

A Survival Guide to Ministry in the Big City

HELP!
I'M AN
URBAN YOUTH WORKER!

A Survival Guide
to Ministry in the Big City

Ginger Sinsabaugh

Youth Specialties

ZONDERVAN

A DIVISION OF HARPERCOLLINS*PUBLISHERS*

Help! I'm an Urban Youth Worker! A survival guide to ministry in the big city

Copyright © 2001 by Youth Specialties

Youth Specialties Books, 300 S. Pierce St., El Cajon, CA 92020, are published by Zondervan Publishing House, 5300 Patterson Ave. S.E., Grand Rapids, MI 49530.

Library of Congress Cataloging-In-Publication Data

MacDonald, Ginger Sinsabaugh, 1961-
  Help, I'm an urban youth worker! : a survival guide to teen ministry in
the big city / Ginger Sinsabaugh MacDonald.
    p. cm.
  ISBN 0-310-23609-6 (alk. paper)
  1. Church group work with teenagers. 2. City churches. I. Title.

BV4447 .M22 2001
259'.23'091732—cd21

20010117560

Unless otherwise indicated, all Scripture quotations are taken from the *Holy Bible: New International Version* (North American Edition). Copyright © 1973, 1978, 1984 by International Bible Society. Used by permission of Zondervan Publishing House.

Web site addresses listed in this book were current at the time of publication. Please contact us via e-mail (YS@YouthSpecialties.com) to report URLs that no longer are operational and replacement URLs if available.

The names of individuals in this book have been changed to protect their real identities.

Edited by Linda Bannan and Dave Urbanski
Additional contributions by Efrem Smith
Cover and interior design by Unidea

Printed in the United States of America

01 02 03 04 05 06 07 / / 10 9 8 7 6 5 4 3 2 1

For courageous lil' Chloe.

Special thanks to my husband, Jeff, as well as the spouses of youth leaders everywhere who support us despite the insanity. Also special thanks to anyone who's ever bought a candy bar to help send a kid to camp.

Contents

Introduction

Breaking Concrete

E bony, a teenager from Chicago's inner city, gave a painfully accurate response when asked about the shootings in suburban high schools across the country. "Teens get shot in my neighborhood all the time. It just not news 'cuz nobody cares."

How true. In many ways, urban youth are cast off, stereotyped, and forgotten.

Maybe you picked up this book because you're an urban youth worker looking for new ideas. Maybe you're a suburban youth worker curious about urban youth ministry. Even if you're a rural youth worker, this book is written with the hope and prayer that God will move in you to help meet the needs of kids where concrete is plentiful but grass and trees aren't.

While Youth Specialties "Help!" books have always been geared specifically to volunteers, this one's a bit different. Because of the lack of resources available specifically for urban youth ministry, *Help! I'm an Urban Youth Worker* is written both for the volunteer and the full-time youth minister in the big city—because in many cases, that's a single individual!

Wherever you're from, remember this: The city is a lot like a teenager—you have to win it from the inside out. And if we can reach kids who reside in the heart of the city and let Jesus change them, they will change the city itself! And when the cities change, everything around them will begin to change, too.

 Kids try to be what they aren't. Urban kids want to be like the suburban kids. Suburban kids want to be like urban kids. Deep down, they're all the same.
—*Theron Forshee, the STEP Foundation, Montgomery, Alabama*

If you're anything like me, you'll find urban youth ministry one of the most rewarding adventures in life. It increases your faith, your patience—and your tolerance for the taste of hot sauce on potato chips! You'll meet teens who'll touch your life as much as you touch theirs. But you might not know where to start or have a clue how to break concrete in urban ministry: *What are the kids like? Can I really make a difference? Why am I here?*

Relax.

While experience truly is the best teacher, hopefully this survival guide will shorten your learning curve as well as keep you encouraged.

Exactly What *Is* Urban Youth Ministry?

Whatever your preconceptions are, throw 'em out!

For starters urban youth ministry isn't about dealing with

The Dos
of Urban Youth Ministry

- Do go into urban ministry with a long-term vision.
- Do focus on building relationships.
- Do focus on the things you can change, not the things you can't.
- Do come with an endless supply of patience.

 ## The Don'ts
of Urban Youth Ministry

- Don't expect overnight results.
- Don't confuse success with attendance.
- Don't feel guilty that you can't do it all.
- Don't freak when you see one of your regulars on *COPS*.
- Don't give up!

one skin color or nationality. If you're in Chicago, urban youth ministry could mean dealing with Romanian immigrant teens or "shorties" (younger kids) in the projects. In Los Angeles, it could mean dealing with Korean or African-American gangs. In Miami, it could mean working with Puerto Ricans, Cubans, and other Latinos (each with unique cultural differences). In other places, it could mean working with runaways, teen moms, or all of the above.

Over the years I've worked with a melting pot of nationalities in various inner-city neighborhoods in Chicago, all of them with their own challenges. My stomping ground du jour is Cabrini Green, one of the nation's poorest housing projects—just six blocks from one of the nation's richest neighborhoods. One side of the street is the land of blue bloods, on the other side—the land of bloodshed.

Sometimes, urban youth ministry is viewed as emergency aid to the part of town where crack houses have yet to be replaced with trendy coffee shops and galleries. This kind of thinking can do more harm than good. You'll find urban youth ministry is not so much about repairing buildings as building relationships.

If I Can Do It, Anybody Can

I didn't grow up in inner-city Chicago, but in a small farm town with one stoplight and a lot of fruit trees. No gang-banging, just cow tipping. It was a real-life Mayberry. You didn't lock your doors at night, and you were never hassled by homeless people. In the early '80s, I left this rural utopia for an advertising job in Chicago. Somewhere between commercial breaks, I gave up the ad career for youth ministry. Go figure. It started the night I ended up in Chicago's Cook County jail on my birthday. (Don't panic—I was new to the city and didn't want to spend my day alone, so I joined my church's jail outreach.) Talk about a birthday surprise! It wasn't at all like the jail on *The Andy Griffith Show*. The halls stunk of Pine-Sol and stale cigarettes. There was more graffiti on the inmates' bodies than on the walls. And the inmates were all teens. I and my small town naiveté were expecting to

Don't romanticize urban youth ministry—have a heart for urban youth and their families. Consider the story of Jesus and the Samaritan woman in John 4. We can learn a lot about going into the city from this exchange.

Verse 4 says, "Now he had to go through Samaria." This is key. Jesus had to go to Samaria because he was *called* there. He couldn't avoid it. Journeying to Samaria was literally part of Jesus. Therefore, you should only go into urban youth ministry because you're called—because you can't avoid it in your soul, because you won't have rest in your spirit until you're used by God to transform young lives in the city.

Jesus went to Samaria to break down walls, to make himself known, and to see lives transformed. This is what should drive us to the city, too. Other reasons include breaking down walls of poverty, broken families, low self-esteem, lack of love, and violence. We ought to go to the city to make Jesus known and to see lives changed through long-term relationships. If this burns in your soul when you look into the eyes of urban youth, then you're qualified. You should go to the city now; and if you're already there, don't leave.

—*Efrem Smith*

see Barney Fife and a friendly town drunk. What a shock!

I continued in this ministry for a few years, but I decided I wanted to reach kids before they wound up behind bars. So before long, I got involved in urban church youth ministry. For the next several years, I worked with some of the finest youth leaders and young people in Chicago. And you know what? I've learned that I'm making a difference. Me. A white girl from Mayberry-land. If I can do it, anybody can.

If you feel called to urban ministry, go for it.

What Makes Urban Youth Ministry So Different?

When urban kids go to camp, their belongings aren't packed in sporty duffel bags, but often in grocery bags. I've met teens whose lives were cut short by bullets or prison sentences. I've attended baby showers where the 14-year-old mother couldn't decide if she wanted to play with the stuffed animals she received or keep them for her baby. Disconnected phones have become my personal pet peeve, driving me to the brink of insanity while I'm just trying to catch up with some kids.

But whoever these kids are, whatever their skin pigments, native tongues, or personality quirks, they have one thing in common with every other kid on the planet: They're kids! Sure they deal with a laundry list of dirty issues, but if you focus on just that, you'll never see how these kids are stars. Think about it. If a kid can make it through an inner-city high school without getting shot, dropping out, or ending up pregnant or in jail, there's nothing he or she can't do!

It's your job to help these kids remember that.

A Lesson from Ancient (Urban) Israel

The best role model for urban ministry came from a place like the 'hood. (Hint: Nobody thought anything good would come from it.)

What Makes Urban Teens Different— (according to youth leaders)

Crumbling homes

Lack of living, breathing male role models

Empty refrigerators

Shortage of self-esteem

Limited experiences outside their neighborhood

Biblical illiteracy

Resiliency to a lot of the above!

What Makes Urban Teens the Same— (according to youth leaders)

They're kids

Their values are set by the media

They're exposed to sex, violence, drugs

They need to belong

They're bored and apathetic

They fear of the future

They're talented and creative

They love pizza

They need Jesus!

Jesus of Nazareth had a thriving urban ministry with only a handful of unpaid volunteers, no video equipment, and definitely no Web site. His audience was poor. He dealt with issues that are alive and well today: poverty, racism, broken homes, and ugly pasts. He hung out with the sexually promiscuous, like Mary Magdalene. He ministered to members of an unpopular Samaritan minority. He showed love to

→ I Got Some Help with This Book!

After umpteen years of experience, I've learned one thing: There's a lot more I don't know than I do know! That's why I contacted veteran leaders across the country to create this book. These Christian leaders are of all ages, all colors, and all backgrounds, and they have all kinds of urban ministries that deal with all kinds of issues. I heard gobs of great stories, wrote down their best advice, and put them all together. So what you have in your hands is a bit of all our expertise, not just mine. Here are a few of those individuals whose input and dedication made this book possible:

Larry Butterfield	Esther Hall	TR Santos
Rudy Carrasco	LaTonya Horton	Brandon Savage
Dan Christie	Phil Jackson	Glen Schriber
Theron Forshee	Joseph Krajnc	William T. Sherrod
Saleem Ghubril	Scott Larson	Efrem Smith
John Green	Danny Lopez	Don Stubbs
Dan Gilbert	Jeff Neven	Dana Thomas
Brad Grinnen	Rosemary Oliver	Keith Wasserman

beggars, lepers, and outcasts. He was even a chaplain of sorts to a dying thief on a cross. Come to think of it, Jesus himself was the son of a teenage mother.

So while this survival guide can offer a few pointers, your best bet for getting a handle on urban youth ministry is to look at Jesus!

Is That It?

In urban youth ministry, you'll deal with many more issues than just ministry. You'll be dealing with high-risk kids—those who're just one mistake away from prison, teen pregnancy, homicide, or dropping out of school.

But you'll discover that tough environments can produce stellar personal qualities. You'll work with teens who're resilient and communicative, and—with your help—they will view their problems as stepping stones to a closer walk with God. Who knows…they just might take over that thriving ministry in the suburbs you just left! 🛑

1

The Volunteer Hunt

Finding volunteers is tough. Finding qualified volunteers is even tougher. And in urban youth ministry, you'll need three times the manpower to keep things running

You can't be an island. You have to build a group.
—*Big Tommy, Streetlight Ministries, Chicago*

smoothly. So where do you find help that you can't afford to hire—or fire?

Variety Is the Spice of Life

Create a team that will bring an assortment of talents, strengths, and ideas to the ministry. Besides, different teens will gravitate toward different leaders. So welcome all colors, all backgrounds, all ages, all zip codes. This will also help teens realize that we're all more alike than we think.

There's No Place Like Home

The best kind of urban youth leaders are indigenous—those who grew up in the very community they're trying to reach. That's the strength of Harambee Christian Center (HCC) in Pasadena, California. ("Harambee" means "let's push together" in Swahili.)

HCC helped transform one of the bloodiest corners in a Latino and African-American neighborhood into a place where kids beat the streets through tutoring, discipleship, and after-school programs. The goal of HCC is to see these kids graduate from college and return to the community as leaders themselves. Now interns from all over the country visit Harambee to learn about its successful form of indigenous ministry.

Recruit adult leaders according to their passions, not according to the traditional needs of the church. When I first looked for youth ministry volunteers at Park Avenue Church in urban Minneapolis, I looked to fill traditional positions. When I met a guy named Ricky, he said he loved DJing in clubs and throwing house parties, but his real passion was using his gifts to build God's kingdom.

When Ricky began to spin records as kids were coming in for youth group, it totally changed the atmosphere of our Wednesday night club. Kids who normally wouldn't come to a church gathering were showing up. Ricky came every week, setting up his sound system and lights. Our youth group became relevant to the urban youth culture around us—because of Ricky's help!

I believe there are a lot of volunteers-in-waiting all around us with abilities to help us reach the urban youth culture in exciting new ways. Just don't limit yourself to obvious volunteers. Maybe you just need a DJ...or a dance teacher...or someone to teach kids how to use hip-hop music to reach their friends for Christ. Recruit volunteers according to their passions.

The urban youth culture is about passion. And the passion of adult volunteer leaders is a key part of your outreach program.

—*Efrem Smith*

Color Not Required

While indigenous leaders are the best, outsiders can work wonders, too. It was a wave hello from "Larry the White Guy" that got Reggie to rethink his life path. Larry, who devoted his life to urban ministry, viewed his lack of pigment as a blessing. Larry believed that no color was a white flag for kids of all colors—not just for kids of one race.

 I'm amazed at what God can do through fools like me who really don't know we're doing!

—*Dana Thomas, director,*
Sunshine Gospel Ministries, Chicago

Reggie—a big, burly, black kid born and raised in the projects—couldn't help but notice Larry in his 'hood: "You don't notice Larry's skin color, you notice Larry." Larry concentrated on just being himself. He was honest about not knowing what it was to live in a gang-infested neighborhood or with a crack addict. But Larry was equally as frank about what he did know—that if Reggie were to drop out of school, this would be the best his life would ever be. Larry was also good for fatherly advice and just playing catch.

While his skin color did close a few doors, Larry's friendly wave hello to Reggie opened a whole lot of windows. So when kids like Reggie were ready to beat the streets, they knew Larry had a helping hand.

100% Authentic

You want leaders who can be real with teens because you're dealing with teens who will be real with them. Urban teens have no problem communicating freely about hard-core issues—gangs, drugs, sex…you name it. You want leaders who won't act holier than thou but will use wisdom to share their own struggles.

0% Dead Weight

The I'll-show-up-when-I-feel-like-it volunteer is best trimmed off your team. Urban kids already have enough adults in their lives who blow them off—from the parent they never see to the youth pastor you're replacing. They need commitment—and you do, too. Other big zeros are the do-as-I-say-not-as-I-do leaders. They can easily lead teens in the wrong direction without even trying. So no matter how desperate you are for volunteers, you're never too desperate to skimp on standards.

Grow Your Own

This process takes years, not just a great experience at summer camp. Teen leaders might be on fire for God one week and gettin' jiggy wit it the next. Or they might use their leadership status as an excuse to skip school or blow off work. So while teens can be great at reaching other teens on their own

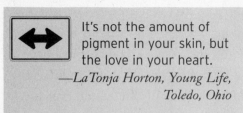

It's not the amount of pigment in your skin, but the love in your heart.
—*LaTonja Horton, Young Life, Toledo, Ohio*

turf—and can be a tremendous help with the shorties—allow them to simply be teens at your meetings. They'll be the pick of the crop for someone else later.

Try the 'Burbs

One of the best places to find help is the 'burbs. Suburban youth group leaders know that volunteering can actually empower teens to overcome their own problems. (Suburban teens have issues, too!) They want to help, and many of them actually prefer assisting outreach projects as opposed to summer camps.

Or you can check out churches from higher-income areas in your city. They have willing volunteers—but not necessarily a cause. So find a church that'll partner with you for fundraisers, construction projects, or whatever needs to be done for your youth group. In return, your kids can help these churches with their big projects. You'll be surprised at how much you both need each other!

My first experience in urban youth ministry was working for Hospitality House Boys and Girls Club in inner-city Minneapolis. I was placed in a church with a gym in the basement, and my assignment was to reach out to boys in the neighborhood. I thought having a gym with a basketball court was a great draw to reach boys in the 'hood. I came up with all kinds of ideas on how to use the gym—3-on-3 tournaments, 5-on-5 tournaments, a summer league, and so forth. My dream became a nightmare the first night I opened the gym. It rained, and I realized there was a leak in the ceiling right above center court. Here we were, trying to play basketball with a water puddle on the court. Boy, was I angry! "How could this happen?" I wondered.

But while I was busy being angry, I didn't notice that the students themselves didn't mind the puddle of water at all. They played on anyway, laughing and making new friends with people they didn't know. Once I noticed what was going on, I grabbed a bucket and put it at center court, and I joined the game. I had become so concerned about the gym that I almost lost the opportunity to build relationships.

That group of young boys that night became my first Bible study group. One of them named Calvin is now working with me on staff this summer at Park Avenue. To see him now as an adult, pouring his life into children in our neighborhood, shows me the importance of building relationships over having relationships with buildings.

—*Efrem Smith*

Beware of One Night Stands

While some churches want to help, make sure they're not doing it to clean their consciences. "In-and-out" ministries are appreciated more once they're "out." No teenager wants to feel like someone else's good-will project. Building lasting relationships with sister ministries is more important than building anything else. Your teens will remember sincerity a lot longer than the freshly painted walls.

Check with Your Local Bible College

Many Bible colleges require students to take internships or help ministries as part of their education. So why not see if they can help out with yours? Bible college students can help with music, create newsletters, tutor, lead Bible studies, or just shoot hoops. Plus, colleges and universities are likely to have Christian organizations such as InterVarsity or Campus Crusade that you can tap into as well.

Check Your Pews

You'll find pew warmers are good for more than checking their watches during service. They're your future tutors, referees, chaperones, drywallers, and more. Just finding someone to bring kids home

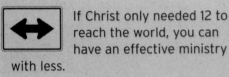

If Christ only needed 12 to reach the world, you can have an effective ministry with less.

—*Efrem Smith*

on a regular basis can help out tons. The grayer the hair is, the greater the commitment.

Most Important, Check References

When you get someone who's interested in volunteering, don't just ask for references—check them. While this may take a little time now, it won't compare to the headaches you'll save later. If they were at other churches before yours, talk to those pastors or lay ministers. If you've never seen them before, find out where they've been. If there's anything questionable in their pasts, decline their offer. It's your job to put the teens' interests over that adults' desire to help. Because the only thing worse than being shorthanded is having a volunteer who shouldn't be one. 🛑

2

His House Rules

I n urban youth ministry, you deal with unique discipline challenges. For starters, many teens don't get discipline at home, so keeping them in line at youth group will take time, effort, and patience. Your inner-city youth group will resemble the audience of *The Jerry Springer Show* a lot more often than what your pastor sees on Sunday mornings! Some kids are gang-bangers, some deal drugs, many are sexually active, and all complain about being bored.

 Kids love the flash. You will have kids quit. Tragedies, pregnancy from good kids, hyped one year then out the door the next. Don't let go of these kids. Hold on!

—*Danny Lopez, youth pastor, Evangel Assembly of God, Chicago*

Here are some things to remember when setting up rules for your youth group:

Rules for Them

Be clothes-minded. Since caps, bandanas, and other headgear are popular gang-wear, a no-headwear policy is a good rule of thumb. Make your youth center a gang-free zone.

> Don't go to extreme with this issue. Not all the kids are wearing bandanas or caps because they're in gangs. They're fashion statements in the hip-hop community as well as in the suburbs. Maybe the focus should be more on the spirit of the environment they walk into (your youth room) as opposed to the wardrobe they walk in with. Allowing kids to come as they are may be a great opportunity to have serious discussions on dress in the 'hood.
>
> —*Efrem Smith*

Don't utter the gutter. Swearing is only the tip of the iceberg when it comes to negative language. Many kids may not even be aware of their language. With girls, remind them matter-of-factly that "language like that takes away from their beauty." With guys, just tell them to "rewind" and have them repeat whatever they said with a better choice of words. Cut-down humor, such as "yo mama" jokes, work against building up the group. Even if the words don't hurt your ears, they can hurt a teen's heart. Cut all forms of trash talk from your youth group.

> *Out of the same mouth come praise and cursing.*
> *My brothers, this should not be.*
>
> —James 3:10

Stay unplugged. Bringing headphones and portable CD players to the youth center only brings problems. They're items other kids will walk out with or use to tune you out. Keeping secular music and media out of the youth center, bus trips, and camps is a good idea, too. Your time with them might be the one time their ears are open to God, so don't close them with such distractions.

Just checking. A mandatory coat check can deter teens from packing weapons and unwanted items under bulky layers. But to get this to work, you have to be diligent and consistent (i.e., don't do it with only some students but not others). Checking coats also keeps teens from walking off with others' belongings.

 Don't feel bad if some teens bust out of your meeting halfway through. If they don't want to be there, don't force them. There will be a day when they do stick around.
—*Rudy Carrasco, associate director, Harambee Christian Family Center, Pasadena, California*

Bounce off and bounce out. Since many urban teens are from homes with no breathing room, expect them to bring a lot of extra energy to meetings. In other words, they'll be bouncing off the walls. So be sure to give them time to spaz out! A few crowd breakers could do the trick. But if during the meat of the meeting students are keeping others from listening, ask them to leave. Remind them, though, it's their behavior—not them personally—that's not appreciated.

When they give you lip…and they will. Cocky attitudes are usually a shield and may take several months to come down. So until then, know that when students give you lip and a bit of head bobbin', you most likely hit a nerve. Try to pick up the conversation later, beginning it with something like, "I was really concerned about you the other night when…" If a teen really explodes, help her calm down, reminding her to "take a deep breath" or "chill out." Whatever you do, don't freak out, too!

You talk, you walk. This rule always works. Many urban teens are ride-dependent. So if a teen continues to talk through your lesson, remind him that he can walk home.

Crack down on gum. Chips, gum, and other teen snacks can get out of hand. So why not take a gum offering? Send a lined offering basket around your youth room. Ask your students to donate their gum, chips, or anything else they'd be munching, chomping, or cracking during the meeting. Send this flavorful offering to a junk food-deprived youth group in China—or just savor the lack of edible distractions while you teach.

I disagree with this point. Providing food, soda, and candy is a great way to help build community. It's also a great way to recruit volunteers who aren't up-front people, but who would run a snack bar at a weekly club event. We offer candy, food, and snacks at our weekly club meeting. I've seen a number of suburban ministries that do this, so why stereotype the urban kids? What's the difference between a suburban kid on sugar and an urban kid?

—*Efrem Smith*

If they're high, say goodbye. If a kid comes to your meeting high or drunk, don't trip out. Call the parents and have them do a pick up. Make sure the student understands he won't be welcome to youth group if it happens again. And if you have to confiscate alcohol or drugs during a meeting or outing, tell the guilty parties, "If you want to stay, these substances can't." (And if they choose your outing over the drugs or alcohol, don't be surprised if they expect you to give the stuff back to them after the meeting! By the way...don't.)

When there are fights... Dan Gilbert is no lightweight, especially when it comes to breaking up a brawl. He's the 260-pound package of muscle that helps manage Moody Bible Institute's Solheim Center, which is often used by various urban ministries. So Dan has to know what to do when things get ugly—and know it fast. Here's his advice:

When you know the teens, jump in and break them up. You've earned the right to do so. First use your voice, and then use your muscle. Get as many leaders as possible to help. Keep the involved teens apart until they cool down. When they are no longer explosive, whether it's that evening or the next week, discuss the incident with each teen.

When you don't know the teens, don't take chances. Call 911 as soon as possible. Be on the lookout for weapons. The same is true if the fight turns into a group brawl. Get uninvolved teens away from the trouble quickly.

Never fly solo. Because fights do happen and get ugly fast, it's important never to be in a situation where you're the only leader, especially if you're female and especially when there are unfamiliar faces in the crowd. Yank someone (preferably *big* and *male*) from the main sanctuary to help if you if necessary. Don't allow unfamiliar faces on special outings if you are short on volunteers. A cell phone can literally be a lifesaver. Above all, don't allow a situation in which you can't get help when you need it.

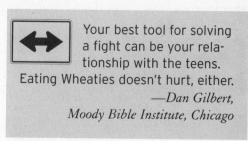

Your best tool for solving a fight can be your relationship with the teens. Eating Wheaties doesn't hurt, either.
—*Dan Gilbert,*
Moody Bible Institute, Chicago

In all situations, stay calm, but be forceful. A strong, commanding voice can work wonders. If the teens are hotheads, be stern. If they have decent temperaments, try to reason. If a blunt instrument (such as a baseball bat or brick) is being used, first demand that the weapon be put down. If that doesn't work, try (with the help of several others) to seize the weapon. If the weapon is a gun or knife, call 911 immediately.

Always trust your gut. If an activity (like a game of pick-up) escalates tempers, end it. Putting your arm around a heated teen and instructing him to "cool down," "chill," or "let's walk" can stop a fight before it starts. Remember, it's a privilege to attend your meetings, not a right.

Rules for You

Be a positive role model. Always use encouraging language, even when it comes to discipline. Don't overuse "don't." Be sure to separate behaviors from students. And be quick to tell teens what they've done well, even if it's just sharing smiles. You will never be guilty of handing out too much praise.

Remember the "men" in "mentor." Many urban teens aren't used to positive male role models. So guys, you can wind up with a lose-lose situation, believe it or not. The students might hate you because you represent their fathers, and they might also hate you because you represent the father they never knew—the father who ran out on them. You have to give these teens time to gain your trust. Work with them, not against them, to overcome each obstacle. But most important, let them know you're on their side.

 The key to cutting-edge ministry is to think small. Let kids disciple kids. Christ only worked with twelve.

—*Efrem Smith*

Read between the lines. Unfortunately urban teens may not have adequate reading skills. Some may not know how to read at all. So calling on students to read out loud is not a good idea. Not only would some be horrified, others might make fun of their efforts. To avoid embarrassment, always ask for volunteers to read.

Think small. Don't feel bad if only three teens show up—even if that's a good day. Remember it's not the number of kids but the number of changes within the kids you're mentoring. One-on-one relationships are what it's all about. You'll always have more than enough to deal with.

Break the broken pattern. These teens are used to inconsistency in every area of their lives. When you plan something for them, they will

really believe in this point. One of the most important things that Bart Campolo—my youth leader—did wasn't a big event, but the relationship building he did with a few. Every Tuesday at 3:15 p.m., Bart would pick up me and three other guys from North High School in Minneapolis and take us to Burger King. He must have known the manager or had some other connection because he always had these free "whopper" cards. So every Tuesday we each got a whopper and a Pepsi; then we would study the Bible together, pray, and talk about what was going on in our lives. This is what I remember most about youth ministry. Bart could have focused on having the biggest youth ministry in Minneapolis, but instead he focused on the impact he could have through long-term relationships with a few. After a while Bart began challenging us to reach out to others. Our youth group began growing because my young peers and I began to reach out to our friends.

I use the same model now. I don't feel pressure to win every young person in Minneapolis to Christ. I try to focus on a small, core group to really invest my life in, knowing that once they catch the vision, they will reach out to others. But even if they don't, I have the opportunity to see spiritual fruit develop through long-term relationships with a few kids who really have access to my life.

—Efrem Smith

look forward to it, no matter how insignificant it might seem to you. Keep your commitments with them. Don't say you will if you won't.

Tailor canned material. Premade lessons are great, but just like that premade potato salad you can buy at the deli, they need your own finishing touches. If not, they could be too sweet for your audience. Take time to customize workbook lessons to meet the unique needs of your urban teens. Put at least as much time into the lesson as the amount of time teens will be sitting in front of you. Demonstrate in real ways that the lesson is especially for them.

Urban youth ministry is incarnational and relational. The key word is *with*. You hang with them; you live with them. Christ is with you, and you are with them.

—*Glen Shriber, Urban Impact,*
New Orleans

Never let them know you don't know what you're doing. The secret of keeping control is acting like you have it, even if you don't. Keep your cool if your guest speaker didn't show up or your lesson bombed. And don't look intimidated by Tito's guest with the missing eye and tattoos, either. Remember, you can do all things through Christ who strengthens you. (Or Christ can do all things through you, if you let him.)

Fewer rules = more control. Jesus had only one golden rule, which made it simple to remember. You can encompass thousands of dos and don'ts with three simple expectations: Listen to leaders, respect property, leave bad attitudes at home. 🛑

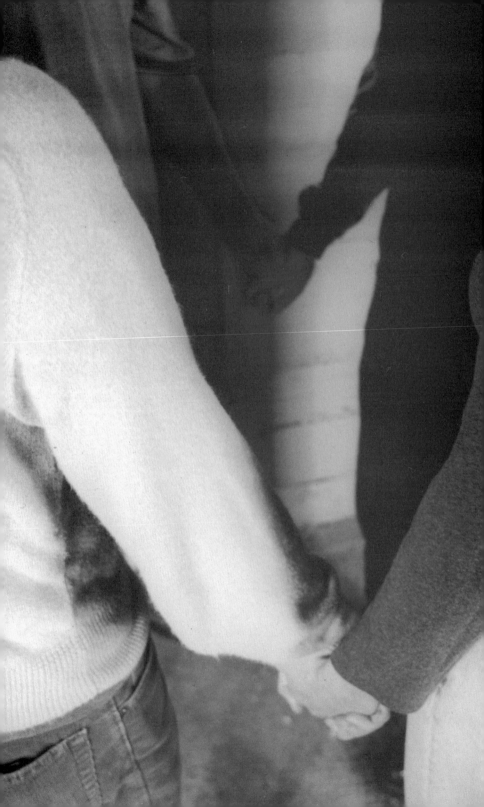

3

Meeting Makers and Breakers

Start with activities and worship that are right for your group, not somebody else's. Next, use lessons that reach your teens where they are, not where your pastor wishes they were. And last but not least, create an environment where teens would rather be than on the streets. Here are some suggestions regarding crowd breakers and meeting makers:

Rethink Worship

If you're blessed with teens who love to shake tambourines and sing in the church choir, you're among the fortunate few. Most urban teens would rather wrestle a pit bull than open their mouths. So do you cut out worship to cut out their complaining? Never. The Psalms tell us to make a joyful noise unto the Lord. As an urban youth pastor, it's your job to discover what that noise is.

Clap your hands, all you nations; shout to God with cries of joy.
—Psalm 47:1

Poetic Justice

Challenge some students to write poems about God. Ask them to read

Remember, it takes relationships to make an urban youth ministry successful—not programs. Am I saying out with programs? No. I am saying, however, that relationship building with youth ought to be the cornerstone of your ministry. Think about Jesus's ministry. Was it about relationships or programs? Bart Campolo was my youth pastor when I was in high school. When I think back on those years, I don't remember a lot of the programs, but I remember that relationship. I remember being at a coffeeshop talking to Bart about dating. I remember him taking me to pass my driver's license test so that I could drive my date to the prom. I remember how every Tuesday Bart would pick up me and three other guys after school, take us to Burger King, and lead us in a Bible study. Because of this relationship building, we began to share Christ with others, and this led to growth in our youth group—and then that led to the need for programs.

—*Efrem Smith*

their poems as part of a worship meeting. But don't stop there. Find some more talent to put the poems to a beat. Writing raps about the Word works well, too.

Put a Big Squeeze on Prayer

Prayer can be an awkward time. Take the pressure off teens by having a "squeeze prayer." Have everyone hold hands in a big circle. A leader starts the prayer (out loud) and then squeezes the hand of the teens on either side of her. If they don't want to pray, they just squeeze on.

Team Up

Sometimes the most fatal mistake we can make in urban ministry is viewing the church down the street as a rival. Urban teens cannot attend too many youth groups! Pool together with area youth groups for big extravaganzas or for nights when you have special speakers or are dealing with a heavy topic such as AIDS. By working together, you can beat your only real competition—the street.

Crowd Breakers

They're a great way to burn energy and have a lot of fun. Your best bet is to invest in a few books on crowd breakers and activities, or just watch a lot of *The Three Stooges*. A good rule of thumb? The louder, the better.

With urban teens, it's important to find crowd breakers that help them lower their tough façade (i.e., make 'em laugh). This might take a while at first, as they'll be very insecure and might be afraid of looking "uncool." So make sure no one's getting laughed at and every-

 The lack of video equipment means you'll have to rely on more creativity or activities, as well as activities that run on energy, not batteries.
—*Dana Thomas, Sunshine Gospel Ministries, Chicago*

I totally agree with this point. No urban youth worker should do youth ministry alone or on an island. In Minneapolis, a group of us have formed a group called Urban R.E.C.L.A.I.M. It consists of weekly meetings for prayer and fellowship, as well as for brainstorming ideas and opportunities for partnership and collaboration. This group consists of church youth pastors, parachurch urban directors, and others who may not work for ministries but are Christians working with youth.

—*Efrem Smith*

one is enjoying the fun. Once they laugh and put down their guards, your teens won't be as tough later on.

Burn Energy, Don't Burn Out

No doubt basketball and other games will be popular with your teens. Still, you want to rotate activities to avoid turning a favorite into the same ol' same ol'. So when you plan your next meeting's activities, ask yourself when was the last time you did something for the first time? If you can't remember, it's time to try something new.

If You Swim, You'll Sink

As fun as it can be, swimming might not be the best activity for an urban youth group. Lots of urban teens don't know how to swim, so water activities could be dangerous or just belly flop. Instead get a show of hands of who can swim before heading to the pool. What could make a good activity is to organize for some real swimming lessons. Not only will you be teaching teens a skill that could save their lives someday, you'll make a big splash as well.

Other Meeting Makers

More than an activity or lesson, your teens need a place where they

Jesus had his some of his greatest impact with the disciples during teachable moments. The woman caught in adultery was a teachable moment. The feeding of the 5,000 was a teachable moment. Teaching a kid to swim, play hockey, put up a tent, bike 50 miles, canoe—all of them are teachable moments in urban youth ministry.

—*Efrem Smith*

feel like they belong…a place where they feel like somebody, period. This atmosphere will be your biggest defense against gangs. T-shirts go a long way in creating that feeling; so if you can scrape up the cash, go for it. If that seems like pie in the sky, try these suggestions:

Homey pages. Here's a great way to gather the info you need about teens while creating a book just for them. All you need is a three-ring binder, some clear acetate sleeves, and a "Who Am I?" questionnaire that you hand out to each teen. Ask for stuff you need (addresses, phone numbers, guardian names) and the stuff they care about (favorite junk food, favorite TV show, what they want to be). Also include a place for them to put their photos and autographs. As the year goes by, add pages with highlights from outings and their view-

> Comparing scars is a good activity!
> —*Scott, SLAM! Youth Ministries, Chicago*

points on certain issues. Save these books and bring them to every meeting. Your kids will enjoy looking at the pictures and reading about each other.

Make somebody's birthday. Youth group is place where you can have your own special traditions, rituals, and holidays. Start with celebrating birthdays. Since urban teens might not have blowout birthday parties at home, your celebration will have even more importance. Bring a cake, and they will surely bring their friends. Celebrating other events, from someone pulling up her grades to a funeral for that once-pesky cockroach, can be fun.

Building self-esteem from scrap. If you tackle this issue, you'll knock out a whole lot of others as well. And all you need are pieces of scrap paper. Start by writing a teen's name on a piece of scrap paper.

Two traditions that really have had an impact in our youth group are house parties and "ghettolympics." The house parties began when parents allowed us to throw monthly alternative social gatherings in their homes. It was a great community-building event for the teens, but it gave parents a different perspective on urban youth ministry as well—and was a way for them to be involved.

Ghettolympics is the name of our weekly competition-icebreaker during Wednesday night club. It's funny how this came about. I was having a hard time getting the youth to participate in games, but just naming one game ghettolympics got them involved. Then later on, when I started a meeting with food, a girl yelled out, "What about ghettolympics? It's not the same without ghettolympics!"

—*Efrem Smith*

Pass the paper around the youth group, having everyone write one nice thing about that person. Finally give it to the teen and sign it, "From Us to You." Do this for everyone in your youth group. You

STILL STUCK FOR SOMETHING TO DO?

One of the best things we've done was help people who were stuck in the snow after the blizzard of '79. The activity of the night was to find five people who were stuck, help dig them out, and come back and talk about it. The teens eventually pushed out 350 cars. The teens got used to helping people and looked for chances to help. They did not accept money. The legendary shovel is still around, with a notch in if for every car it pushed out.

—*former youth pastor, Chicago*

won't find any of these papers crumbled on the youth center floor. Seeing and reading positive things about themselves is an incredible experience for kids.

Turn your *youth* group into an *us* group. Youth group is like everything else in life—it's only as exciting as we make it. So make it a place

D on't just recognize that teens can't read; do something about it. I believe urban youth ministry should be holistic. We ought to develop a ministry that reaches the whole person—spiritually, academically, and socially. I know this sounds like a lot, but it doesn't have to be. It could be as simple as developing a homework room at your church, having alternative dance parties on Friday nights, or starting a community basketball league. This is also a great way to get more people invested in urban youth ministry. Some people may not feel comfortable leading a Bible study, but could read with a kid every week, or donate a computer to start a computer center, or provide food for a dance party.

Growing up, I remember a church called Tabernacle Baptist. It would have youth dance parties on Friday nights. I couldn't believe my eyes when I first walked into one of these parties. There was a guy playing music, church people treating me like I really belonged in church, and older women cooking chicken dinners and mixing fruit drinks. That experience changed my whole outlook on church and God. It also provided a social alternative that kept me out of trouble. Urban youth ministry must be more than just "receive Jesus right now"; it ought to be about the holistic development of youth. I believe that Jesus cares about kids being able to read so they develop positive relationship and community-building skills.

—*Efrem Smith*

for your students to celebrate their diversity—from their ethnicities to their talents. Make it a place for them to channel their energy, creativity, and ideas. Let them feel responsible for successes as well as flops. Get those graffiti tag artists to design a T-shirt or banner. Put those rappers in charge of music. Put the kid who's always cutting up in charge of crowd breakers. Encourage some of the shy kids to start a newsletter-mailer (this not only will build unity; it can help with academic skills). 🛑

4

Nuthin' Like the Benjamins

If you never have enough money or enough Doritos to feed your group, join the club. Money doesn't grow on trees, at least not in big-city neighborhoods. Urban teens live in communities where good jobs are scarce, and often the only people bringing home the bacon are the drug dealers. And meanwhile, you can't find the money to send your students to summer camp! But a shortage of money could give you the opportunity to teach your kids something money can't buy—the value of hard work.

Nix "No Strings Attached"

Resist the urge to give things to teens with no strings attached. Even in dire economic situations, teens won't value things they didn't work for. Allow them to earn these things in creative ways—good youth group attendance, helping with worship, or just pulling up grades. It will decrease the chances that you'll be left with 20 Lakers tickets or 20 empty bunks at camp or 20 new Bibles left in the rain. Besides the only thing harder than getting kids to do a little work for pay is explaining to Mr. Generous why his donation went to waste.

Gimme a Break

If you're tired of teens coming up to you and saying, "Gimme a dollar," you'll love quoting 2 Thessalonians 3:10. It reminds us, "If a man will not work, he shall not eat"—even if it's extra hot cheese curls. So require teens to earn that dollar in fun ways. Make them memorize a verse, clean up the youth center—or some aspect of their behavior. It's a great way to remind students that you had to work hard for that money, and so should they.

Cash It or Stash It

If cash is hard to come by, why not create your own? Replace your current point system with "Cash It or Stash It." Teens can earn "cash" by doing anything you would normally give points for—verse memorization, doing well in school, bringing a friend to group, et cetera. Then teens can cash it in for soda pop, outings, or camp. If you have a computer, you can make a dollar template with a basic graphics program and scan photos of your teens to replace presidents' portraits. Cash It or Stash It will take the pressure off you keeping track of points, and it will teach teens how to manage money they rarely have.

When Work Is the Pits

Growing up in small town where my grandparents had a farm gave me no choice when it came to work. I was brought into this world to pick cherries. I picked so many that I still have a hard time eating them to this day. But picking cherries, climbing trees with a bucket attached to my belt, getting sticky from the heat, and having my hands stained from cherry juice—and even my

 These kids are deeply imbedded to rely on handouts. We have to help break the cycle.
—*Theron Forshee, S.T.E.P. foundation, Montgomery, Alabama*

back hurting from the bucket—motivated me to continue my education. Every time I wanted to drop out, all anyone had to say was "cherries." So remember, even jobs teens detest now can help them avoid life in the pits. Be an advocate of hard work.

Break the Mold, Not the Bank

While car washes and spaghetti dinners are excellent ways to raise funds, other methods can earn money as well as raise awareness of your ministry. Here are a few examples of urban fundraisers that raise attention as well as cash:

Uncandy sale. Here's a good alternative to the candy sale where no one eats up the profits. Instead of selling chocolate, why not have teens pledge to give up chocolate? Have teens to give up candy, chips, or soda pop for a designated amount of time and get sponsors for this incredible effort. Getting students to abstain from munching in the sanctuary is always a good thing, and you'll have many members who would gladly give to your cause.

Rule of thumb for sticky fingers. Avoid fundraisers that require teens to collect large sums of money. Even if your students might be honest, other family members might not think twice about dipping into that envelope of earnings. One teen's camp fund went up in smoke because her mother used it to support her crack addiction. Other fundraising efforts can supply more fun and a lot less headache.

A bake sale that went to the dogs. Here's one where a youth group was barking up the right tree. With the popularity of canine creatures in Chicago's more affluent neighborhoods, Streetlight Youth Ministry made homemade dog biscuits to sell at a summer fair. All it needed was a dog biscuit recipe and permission to use the church kitchen to bake them. The kids even included fortunes that read, "You will discover a new fire hydrant" and "There will be many wondrous smells in your future." Not only did the fundraiser make the most of a current trend, the dog lovers were glad to give to a good local cause.

Bulletproof beans. In the heart of one of our country's biggest housing projects, a farmer figured that a string bean could save a child's life (i.e., teach a child the skills of gardening, and he will have a positive alternative to hanging on the streets.). But the idea grew

Great point here, but keep this in mind, too: You shouldn't look at alternative means of fundraising just because you're afraid your kids might steal. That kind of thinking stereotypes urban youth and also assumes suburban youth workers don't have to worry about kids stealing—and you know that's not true! Maybe the reason I feel this way is because I wasn't always an urban youth pastor—at one point in my life, I, too, was an urban teenager. And so, when I look at urban youth, many times I see myself! I remember the needs I had when I was a kid. And I remember what kinds of adults I wanted in my life—and how I wanted to be perceived by them. I certainly didn't want them thinking I'd take things that didn't belong to me!

The reason you should look for alternative fundraising is because fundraising is an opportunity to learn big life lessons. Many urban youth and their families don't feel empowered. Many live rental lifestyles and don't own very much at all. Fundraising is a chance to develop leadership and ownership skills in your students.

—*Efrem Smith*

even bigger. This "project produce" was sold to the hottest local restaurants, and the owners delighted in helping this urban venture. The kids not only raised beans and curly endive but public interest as well.

Ridin' the gravy train. The sign-my-sponsor-sheet-and-that's-it-athons can cause more headaches than they're worth—and they teach your students nothing. One of my "good" students once asked church members for $200 in pledges for camp when only $100 was needed—he looked at asking for additional pledges as an easy way to make some fast cash. So think twice about do-nothing sponsorships. They do nothing in the long run.

Take stock in your youth. Here's a good alternative to do-nothing-a-thons. Instead of students asking for donations toward an upcoming camping trip, ask adults to buy stock in the teens. Fake stock certificates are created on a computer, and teens sell stock for a dollar a share. After the teens return from camp, a stockholders' meeting is held. Instead of boring annual reports, the stockholders see a true return on their investments. The kids show slides and photos of camp and give each attendee a stockholders' report that includes highlights of camp along with a thank-you note.

Start a business. One urban ministry in Memphis didn't stop with car washes. Instead, it created its own detailing business. Why? By teaching business skills to youth, the church helps them learn how to handle money and prepare for the future. Along with car detailing, this youth group also mows lawns. But the money doesn't all go toward happy meals. This money is saved, the kids invest in one stock, and those profits go back into the business. Wow! The ministry also has been successful in finding mentors in the business community for these kids. Hopefully, when these teens become successful in their careers, they won't escape to the suburbs but will stay in the urban context.

When you care enough to support the very best. UrbanPromise Ministries in Camden, New Jersey, has a great way to earn money for camp and after-school programs. Kids design, print, and sell greeting cards. And they don't simply sell these cards to nice old ladies, either. Big corporations like to buy them, too.

Here's how the cards are created: At camp or after-school activities, contests are held to decide which students' designs will be used for the cards. And it's not easy picking just one winner. After the top few designs are selected and orders are taken, the cards are printed at their presses.

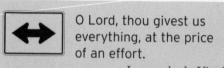

O Lord, thou givest us everything, at the price of an effort.
—*Leonardo da Vinci*
Can I have a dollar?
— *Leonardo da Teen*

While you may not have access to your own printing press, you very well may have access to stellar artists. Your local copy shop should be able to print simple designs or will know a printer that can. Just be sure to use a nice quality paper. For more info, surf to the UrbanPromise Ministries Web site, www.urbanpromiseusa.org, or write to UrbanPromise Ministries at 3700 Rudderow Avenue, Camden, N.J. 08105.

Get a Little Bit Back

Every dollar your teens spend goes into somebody else's pocket—and think of whose pockets they are: McDonald's, Burger King, Tower Records, the Gap, Borders, Pizza Hut, Sega, and Nintendo. So why not get these companies to give back to the hands that feed them? Many national fast-food chains give regularly to groups just like your

Recruit adult leaders according to their passions, not according to the traditional needs of the church. When I first looked for You'll be surprised at the number of people who'd love to invest in the lives of urban teens. The problem is that we need more urban youth workers with a vision for holistic urban youth ministry. You see, most adults who don't feel comfortable leading Bible studies or Sunday school classes don't believe there are places for them in urban youth ministry—but this is far from true.

We limit the impact the urban church can have on young lives when we continue to push only traditional ministry methods. A guy named Steve who volunteers in my youth group started The Inventors Club. He teaches young people how to do things like taking apart CB radios and putting them back together and installing new telephone systems in the church. These kinds of activities instill developmental, leadership, and entrepreneurial skills in young people. Then they begin to dream not just about what they can become, but what they can accomplish and achieve right now. This also creates new and creative ways to develop fundraisers beyond the traditional car wash or a hot dogs and chips sale.

—*Efrem Smith*

urban youth group. If they aren't doing so locally, you might try their national headquarters. But don't stop with a value meal. Product manufacturers from cereal to fabric softeners want to make inroads into ethnic markets, and they know the church is a good place to reach these groups. So if your local pizza shop can't help pay your youth group's way to camp, it might supply the snacks. Also, try your local grocery store. Helping your cause can also help them down the road.

Putting Our Money
Where Our Mouths Are

You can buy teens nacho chips or teach them the skills they need to buy their own. Remember—fundraisers raise more than funds. They build unity, raise self-esteem, and teach valuable lessons about goals, planning, and responsibility. They also groom talents and skills that help prepare teens for the future, just in case those NBA offers don't come flying in. Just make sure to keep the fun in fundraiser, and you'll have an activities as popular as camp itself. ⏹

5

Just Trippin'

If you want to break down the walls urban teens put around themselves, there's nothing better than a road trip. Youth leaders around

 The same kids who were gangbanging in the city and used to hearing gunshots all night would freak out at the sound of a cricket!
—urban youth pastor, Memphis, Tennessee

the country agree on the importance of camp, or simply getting teens out of town. You'll discover many urban teens have never even been out of the city! Many have never held a frog, heard a cricket, smelled the wondrous fumes of a skunk—or even gone finch hunting. Along with being an experience teens will remember for years, camp also gives you an environment to break down those tough façades. Here're some things to remember on your next big trip:

Getting There Is Half the Fun

Never underestimate the power of the bus ride. It's discipleship at 55 miles per hour (or faster, depending on where you reside). You can really get to know kids while sitting next to them for 14 hours. Try to hire a driver for your road trips so you can concentrate on doing what you do best—or at least have a few qualified drivers per vehicle. Then keep the radio off and the conversation flowing.

Consent Forms: Don't Leave Home without Them

They're a pain to collect, but nothing near the pain you'll experience without them. Consent forms are a must for any kind of road trip involving teens. Be sure the form includes guardian information, where you're going, when you'll return, an emergency contact number, and a signature of a parent or legal guardian. Don't get lazy on this one.

Some Guidelines for Your Kids

You might think you're oversimplifying information, but you're not. For instance, you might want to warn your students about poison ivy, the origins of certain nighttime sounds, that skunks really do spray, as well as give them the rundown on your curfews. Or you might want to warn them that small-town folk aren't used to seeing a busload of city kids pull into their gas station. Remind them to be polite.

Operation Duffel Bag

One of the best moments of the camp experience is seeing your kids' excitement as they wait to board the bus. One of the worst is watching them tote grocery bags full of clothes instead of regular luggage containers. Enter Operation Duffel Bag. Invite people in your church who sew to make simple duffle bags for the kids that you can pass out as they board the bus. (Hint: Don't limit this activity to women! You can find men, too, who would love to donate their time and scrap material.) And check

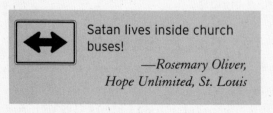

Satan lives inside church buses!
—*Rosemary Oliver,*
Hope Unlimited, St. Louis

sewing classes at your local college and trade schools. It's a great way to share with others what you're doing with your kids.

If Your Vehicle Breaks Down, Don't You Join It!

Even on good days vans and buses break down, don't show up, and get flats. It'll be a test drive for your patience, so make sure you pass. Be sure to have a cell phone and contact numbers to help keep things moving when you're experiencing stalls. Then make the most of that valuable time with your captive teen audience. Have fun, and don't freak.

Leader Focus

Kids Across America

Each year, T.R. Santos has 4,500 miraculous stories to tell about his urban ministry. That's because each year 4,500 kids pass through the gates of Kids Across America (K.A.A.) where T.R. is one of the camp directors. Located near Branson, Missouri, K.A.A. is a five-star Christian athletic camp exclusively for urban teens. T.R. has seen God do some amazing things.

"I get a broad look of what's going on across the country. God uses so many people to touch one life, and I get to see the fruit of others' labors summer after summer." T.R. believes many inner-city kids have a deeper understanding of God's grace because they come from tougher situations than most teens. "It humbles me to see their maturity in faith." But K.A.A. isn't just for kids; it's a place for those whom T.R. calls "frontline warriors," too. "It's where leaders can come to be trained, encouraged, and refreshed before returning to their cities to continue their work." If there's any way you can make it to K.A.A., it's truly worth the trip. (For more info, contact Kids Across America c/o I'm Third Foundation, 1429 Lakeshore Drive, Branson, MO 65616 or surf to www.iamthird.org.)

The Number One Rule: Hold It In

Plan bathroom breaks on long road trips and stick to them. If not, you'll be stopping more than you'll be going (so to speak). Remind teens before you pull away from the church parking lot about your number-one rule. Another word of advice: don't expect the single stall at McDonald's to handle your students. Find those big rest stops with super-sized bathrooms.

Why You Buggin'?

"On one mission trip the roaches were so big that the teens called them Volkswagen bugs," recalls one youth leader. While most insects mind their own business, a swarm of mosquitoes can ruin a good time. So remember to pack extra bug spray—lots of it.

Student Focus
Forget the Free Ride

Jasmine hadn't earned any money for camp yet. The youth leaders—with the little bit of extra money they had in the budget—decided to give her an all-expenses-paid trip to camp. Jasmine was pumped for a while, but at the last minute she decided she didn't feel like going.

Why? Since Jasmine hadn't earned her way to camp, it was no big deal to back out. And since Jasmine's mother didn't make any financial investment, she didn't care much either. So instead of spending an unforgettable week at camp, Jasmine stayed home doing the same ol' same ol', and a camp bunk stayed empty that week.

Requiring a $10 deposit up front (whether they pay in cash or with fundraiser labor) keeps teens from backing out later on, regardless if someone else pays the rest of the way. Having teens personally vested in pricey outings makes for many happy campers.

Tired of Wandering in the Wilderness?

You don't have to do it all yourself. Many camps offer preplanned adventure excursions with all-knowing guides. All you do is bring the kids, and they do the rest. You won't have to worry about renting tents or canoes—or about forgetting the buns. The best thing is that these guides are familiar with the territory, so you won't have to worry about your students getting a glimpse of a nudist colony on the other side of the river. (Yup. It happened to me!) So where do you find these guides? Your favorite traditional camp will probably know of a few outfitters that do this. Or they might even offer packages themselves.

One of the most powerful experiences I've had with my youth group happened on a weekend camping trip. We didn't plan a whole lot of programming. As a matter of fact, the theme for the weekend was "getting to know God." On the second day, we had kids go into the woods alone for two hours with a Bible, a pen, and some paper. All they were told was to get alone with God. I was nervous because a number of my adult leaders thought this would never work with urban youth; boy, were we wrong! When we met that night, the kids shared what they had done. Some had written poetry to God, some wrote rap songs to God, and others wrote plays. That night we had praise and worship time like never before. That weekend was a spiritual turning point in our youth group. We've never been the same.

—*Efrem Smith*

Sista Church

If you can't make it to camp, find a church in the country to hang out with. Just experiencing a town where there's one stop light and no McDonald's will be an eye-opener for urban teens. This could be a low-cost alternative to camp with just as many benefits.

Mission Accomplished

Sometimes the best thing for urban kids in the long run is a short-term mission trip. But forget your passport. Just pack your bags, head to Steel Country, and join The Pittsburgh Project. It gives junior and senior high school students the opportunity to perform hands-on services such as hanging drywall and repairing homes for in-need urban residents. But that's not all. Your students will also participate in worship and small-group discussions when the day's work is done. For more info, contact The Pittsburgh Project at 2801 North Charles Street, Pittsburgh, PA 15214 or surf to www.pittsburghproject.org.

Make It Fun, Not a Prison

Rosemary Oliver knows even a bad camp experience can have a good ending. "There was a kid one summer who was 300 miles from home and wanted to run away from camp. Now that same kid is one my star Bible students—and the first on the camp bus."

But still, the last thing you want is a bad camp experience. On one hand it's important to have rules so students don't, for example, conduct their own lessons on the birds and the bees. On the other hand, sprayed shaving cream doesn't do as much damage as sprayed bullets. So use your discretion and a lot of wisdom. Keep them from attacking raccoons with mace, but let them enjoy the wonders of nature. Camp should be a great experience. Bring your teens into the open air, and watch them open up. 🛑

6

School Daze

Think educational goals are important to your youth ministry? Try telling that to sophomore Tiffany, who can't read that passage in Leviticus because she can't read higher than the third-grade level. Urban teens are failing in school, and the schools are failing them. Many students are simply passed to the next grade, whether they make the grades or not. Others want to do well academically, but their cramped, noisy, and violent homes aren't conducive to studying. Then there's the staggering number of high school dropouts who get the rest of their educations on the streets.

It's hard to do homework in your bedroom when your bedroom is the couch.
—*Naomi, inner-city teen*

While the primary goal of youth ministry is teaching kids the love of Christ, encouraging teens to excel in school puts that love into action. Here are some things to remember when school doesn't rule...

They Won't Go Far on a Dead-ucation

If one of your kids is considering dropping out of school, be frank with her. Make sure she knows there's little chance she'll land a job with no skills or education. And if she believes a GED is an instant answer, tell her to think again. Here's what a GED says about a job applicant: she uses short cuts, she takes the easy way out, she doesn't finish her tasks, and she has no patience. And if one of your teens is banking on being the next Michael Jordan, he needs to understand that a very, very small percentage of superior athletes ever make it to the professional level. Besides, athletic talent is no excuse to blow off the basics. Actually, it's a reason to hit the books harder. What good is a million-dollar contract if you can't read it?

Multiplication Tables for Dropouts

According to some statistics, a high school dropout is:

- 2 times more likely to be unemployed
- 3.5 times more likely to get arrested
- 6 times more likely to be an unwed single parent
- 7 times more likely to be reliant on government assistance

All in all, a dropout is more likely to continue the cycle of poverty.

Prove It to Me!

Okay, so your kids don't believe finding a good job is that difficult? Have them look through the Sunday paper and search for jobs. First, have them look for jobs that appeal to them for any reason, from the job description to the salary. Next, among those positions open, have them look for those that require only a high school diploma. Finally have them look for jobs that sound interesting, pay well, and don't require any special education or experience. It's one thing to tell your kids they won't be able to find a job; it's quite another if they discover that for themselves.

When Juan Can't Read

Teens may not know how to read, but they'll know how to hide it. So if you suspect a problem with illiteracy, confront those kids very carefully. For starters, don't embarrass them in front of others. Even if they can't read, they'll get upset that you think they can't. Devote your efforts to establishing a trusting relationship. Your students must understand that you love them whether they're literate or not. And that'll be the first step in getting them to want to learn how to read!

Bein' Wired Not Required

Even in today's high-tech world, you'll find that computers aren't as important to succeeding in school as your encouragement. While computers (especially donated ones!) are great for some areas of study, they're useless when it comes to motivating teens, encouraging them to solve problems, or praising them when they get the right answer. Never underestimate the power of the pat on the back.

In Tutoring = Out of Trouble

According to popular statistics, the majority of violent crimes committed by teenagers happen between 3 p.m. and 4 p.m.—right after school lets out. That's why after-school tutoring programs can be so effective on many levels. Brothas & Sistas United—a program sponsored by Jesus People USA in Chicago—meets kids right at their schools. Tutors then accompany them to the tutoring center, and there they do homework or get extra help. Along with hitting the books, Brothas & Sistas United offers fun activities, too. But there's a catch: if you don't do your work, you don't get to play. Now why hasn't anyone thought of that before?

The Three Rs of Successful Tutoring

If you want to get your students involved in after-school tutoring at your church, Brothas & Sistas United says successful tutoring programs fail or succeed based on the health of three basic relationships:

1. **Tutor-teacher.** Make sure the tutor has open communication with the teachers. What's going on in the classroom? At what level should these pupils be reading? What are their strengths?

2. **Tutor-parent.** Make sure parents or legal guardians know the tutors' concerns about their children's knowledge gaps and successes. Also warn parents not to revoke youth group privileges for doing poorly in school. This could just spiral into more bad activity.

3. **Tutor-student.** Have tutors stay involved in students' extracurricular activities. Do they play on a school team? Do they sing in your choir? Find out what's at the bottom of their apathetic attitude. Are they failing because they expect to fail, or are they afraid to succeed?

Tutor Check-List

1. **Check your pews.** You might find that those who're interested in tutoring aren't the traditional lock-in volunteers. They might not be comfortable with a basketball, but they're totally cool with biology.

2. **Check your local college.** Education majors might love the chance to create a tutoring program for you.

3. **Check their interests.** Do they love reading or sewing? Math or art? Don't limit your tutoring to the basics. If you have a volunteer who wants to teach photography, let him!

4. **Check the references.** As always…

They'll Make the Time
If You Find the Space

Devote a space in your youth center or church for studying. Make it a place where you'd want to study. Along with tables, you might want to add a few beanbag chairs. If you're blessed with computers, add them too. If this is a multipurpose room, make sure it's student friendly by the time teens arrive. And be sure to remind them that it's a room for studying the Bible, too.

No Show?

Don't be disappointed if the students who need tutoring the most are the ones who never show. You'll discover

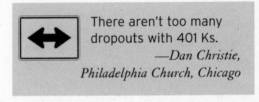

There aren't too many dropouts with 401 Ks.
—*Dan Christie,*
Philadelphia Church, Chicago

that teens who're really lagging academically may avoid your program because they're afraid someone will find out how little they know. Build trust with these kids, and give them time and space.

Gimme 20

If you don't have a tutoring program (yet), why not carve out a time for students to do homework before the youth group meeting? The 20 unused minutes before your activities can really be useful for teens who need a place to study.

Cut Out the Cutting

If you have students who cut their classes, waste no time finding out why. If you discover it's a gang-related problem, notify the school. Let your kids know that some things must be done even if we don't always feel like doing them—Jesus getting nailed to cross, for example. Who could shirk responsibility in the face of that sacrifice?

Whatever you do, work at it with all your heart, as working for the Lord, not for men.

—Colossians 3:23

Be on the Ball with Incentives

When I wrote TV commericials for major cereal companies, I had the opportunity to work with more than flakes. I worked with Michael Jordan and received an autographed basketball. And boy, has that ball come in handy at youth group. The deal is this: whoever graduates high school and goes on to finish college gets the ball. Meanwhile a fellow youth leader got an autographed ball from Kobe Bryant! Between the two of us, we have a lot of boys hitting the books. Whatever these autographed basketballs are worth, they can't compare to those kids getting their diplomas. So work those celebrity connections!

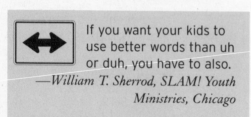

If you want your kids to use better words than uh or duh, you have to also.
—*William T. Sherrod, SLAM! Youth Ministries, Chicago*

The Inside Scoop on Incentives

Whatever incentive you use, be quick to reward teens for their academic efforts. You'd be surprised what a kid would do even for pizza. But don't pay for all of them yourself. Get on the phone and let your community know, from the local professional team to fast-food franchises. They'll be donating goodies before you know it.

Limit Your Use of *Slanguage*

You might be tempted to use street slang to make a point to your group. But it's better to set a good example with your language. By the same token, correct teens' grammar when it needs to be corrected. For instance, have them rewind their "ain't" statements and replay 'em with "is not." It's a friendly, non-critical way of helping them improve their language. And regarding the popular teen response, "Ya know what I'm saying?" answer with, "No, I do not." Raise the bar of what you demand from their lips—and yours.

Youthful Perspectives

In all your activities, encourage teens to voice their opinions, whether you agree with them or not. Many are afraid to voice their opinions and will give you that shoulder shrug response. Don't allow it. Let them know that while it takes courage to think for themselves; if they don't, they're letting someone else do the thinking for them.

It All Adds Up to a Future

A high school diploma won't get your kids into heaven, but it sure comes in handy on this planet. More than anything else, that education breaks the cycle of poverty. It's the one lifelong investment that no one can take away. Still some students are so far behind that they will dodge your efforts to help. While your heart goes out to those kids, put your efforts into the teens who want your help. You can't save the world, but you can help the kids who want to help themselves.

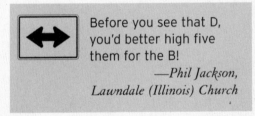

Before you see that D, you'd better high five them for the B!
—*Phil Jackson,*
Lawndale (Illinois) Church

7

Home Is Where the Hurt Is

Youth leaders across the country agree that the biggest problems facing urban kids are often their own families. You really can't call them "broken" families, because many were never whole in the first place. Some seem piecemealed…teens living with an auntie, sister, grandparent, cousin, or all of the above. Others live in terrible conditions—everything from too many people in the house to never enough food on the table. Many parents are

Urban kids do not have stable family lives. Suburban teens might deal with home problems, but it's divorce versus never marred. Many times, in the inner city, the mother is pregnant first, then married, if ever married. There's less of a foundation.

—Larry Butterfield, SLAM! Youth Ministries, Chicago

still kids themselves, hoping that their teens don't make the same mistakes they did—other parents don't care at all.

While you can't fix the problems at home, you can learn how to deal with them.

A Normal Family Isn't the Norm

It won't take you long to learn never to ask a kid, "How are your parents?" If that teen is lucky, he's living with one parent—many are living with relatives. And don't assume that the brothers and sisters at home are the only brothers and sisters. Be sure you're aware of half

Lesson Focus
Joseph's Dysfunctional Childhood

A lesson on Joseph from Genesis lets you point out that a bad home situation doesn't necessarily mean a bad future. Talk about coming from one messed up, made-for-a-TV-talk-show family. Joseph's father married two sisters, giving Joseph 10 envious older brothers—and a lot of frustration. These brothers even plotted to kill him and threw him into a ditch, and Joseph was sold into Egyptian slavery. But he didn't let his family and his past keep him from doing great things. Joseph ended up in Pharaoh's palace, saving his people—as well as his family—during a famine. So a bad home situation doesn't necessarily spit out bad apples. Help teens view obstacles like their home life as stepping-stones to get closer to Christ.

Other imperfect biblical families teens would appreciate:

• Isaac and Ishmael: one father, two mothers (Genesis 21). It's a great lesson for teens in blended families regarding the pains of favoritism. It will open up discussion.

• Cain and Abel: brotherly rivalry turns into murder (Genesis 4). This well-known tale lets teens know that conflict has been around since the first family. Use it to get your students talking about their struggles with siblings.

• Ammon and Tamar: David's son Ammon rapes his sister Tamar (2 Samuel 13). This story lets teens know that abuse happens everywhere, including in the household of a king who believed in God. Assure teens that this type of behavior is wrong—and that Tamar didn't "ask for it."

brothers or sisters, or their parents' other kids. Finally, don't assume that the adult with whom your student lives is the legal

Only one teen in my ministry has both a father and mother at home.
—*youth leader, St. Louis*

guardian. When the family tree has a few twists, expect to be thrown a few curves.

Sons are a heritage from the LORD, children a reward from him.

—Psalm 127:3

When They Don't Miss What's Missing

When single-mother parenting is the norm for urban teens, it's hard to get them to understand that something is missing from their lives. According to one national survey, almost one in five white children, almost one in three Latino kids, and more than half of all African-American youths live in single-parent families.

Teens will be defensive about their home situations, especially if their guardian is a spiritual giant, breadwinner, and stellar example. But regardless of any single parent's strengths, the Bible makes it clear that both a mother and father are important to the kids' development (Ephesians 6:1-4).

The best way to stand in the gap is through your personal example. If you came from a broken home, be candid about how that affected you. Or compare what goes into raising a child to a recipe: forget one key ingredient, and it won't be long before you realize something important was left out of the mixing bowl. (One way to illustrate this point—and similar ones—is by baking a cake without baking powder or making an instant fruit drink without the sugar.)

Spaced Out

Low-rent housing creates problems nearly impossible to fix. Cramped corners can become a pressure cooker for emotions. Imagine if your own couch was actually your bedroom and other people (your own family) wanted to watch TV while you tried to sleep?

Some families are often evicted from their apartments—and might be on the move fairly regularly. Since that can be humiliating for a teen, don't ask why he has a new address.

You'll also have to learn how to stay connected to teens with disconnected phones. A letter in the mail does wonders. Seeing something positive in print is powerful, and they can hang onto your words for a long time.

There are many opportunities to develop a family atmosphere in your youth group. At the same time, though, don't fool yourself into believing that your youth ministry can truly replace the family. It can't! God didn't design things that way. But if your youth ministry can give youth a sense of family, you can teach principles that impact a future generation of mothers, fathers, husbands, and wives. Here are some family-development ideas:

• Share community meals.

• Share how your days went.

• Celebrate birthdays, graduations, sports awards, and other special days or special achievements.

—*Efrem Smith*

Things You Don't Want to Think About

When you combine the stresses of low income with alcohol or drug addiction, you have a volatile recipe for physical or emotional abuse. If you learn that one of your students is being abused physically or sexually, you must report the abuse to either child protective services or social services—look under "Abuse" or "Community Services" in the front of your phone

No matter how messed up the home situation is, you've got to keep in touch with the parents. The bottom line is that the parent is responsible for that kid, not you.
—*Joe Krajnc, Brothas & Sistas United, Jesus People USA*

book. These agencies are filled with trained professionals who deal with these kinds of situations every day. Make sure you assure your student teen this treatment wasn't deserved and that it wasn't his or her fault.

Being available to parents of at-risk kids is crucial work. Don't deal with these kids and ignore the homes they come from. A friend of mine runs a ministry called Christ's Children in inner-city Minneapolis, and one of the things that makes his ministry powerful is his home visits with at-risk kids. Through these visits he's been able to share the gospel with parents and other relatives who never would have set foot inside a church. So don't forget about kids' families!

—*Efrem Smith*

Let the Kid Change the Family

Lots of times parents get introduced (or reintroduced) to church through a child. So you might want to offer programs for parents, too—from retreats to support groups to rediscover-your-youth nights. Even if parents don't show an interest in the youth group, they'll be grateful for the change they see in their teens.

¿No Habla Inglés?

In this world, we care about physical illegitimacy, but we don't care about spiritual illegitimacy. We have to let these kids know who their Father really is!
—*Theron Forshee, the S.T.E.P. Foundation, Montgomery, Alabama*

Are you having a hard time making connections with parents who don't speak English? Start to break down that barrier by offering bilingual consent forms for events like camp. Find someone in your church to help you create a basic template, keep it on file, then update it for various events. It will go a long way toward communicating that your care for their teens.

A Sheltered Life?

If growing up with Grandma in the projects is all a student knows because Mom died of a drug overdose and Dad's in prison, that stu-

After youth group meetings, one girl was dropped off where her mother worked: a strip bar.
—*youth pastor, Chicago*

dent might still be living a (believe it or not) sheltered life. If teens are exposed only to the bad, they don't have much contact with good stuff. Help expose teens to jobs, people, and places outside their immediate neighborhoods. Your routine trip to K-mart might even be a memorable expe-

PARENTAL GUIDANCE SUGGESTED

Orlando, a gangbanging teen from the East Coast, decided he wanted to get on the right track once he got out of jail. But Orlando knew he couldn't do it alone. That's when he came up with an idea. Orlando thought if he could live with a family and do normal things with them, from going to church to eating dinner, he would have a better shot at beating the streets. Orlando described this idea to his church leaders. Though Orlando's idea was interesting, the leadership thought that church would be enough of an influence. So Orlando returned to the streets, and the gang once again became Orlando's family—but only for a short while. Orlando was found one day with a bullet in the back of his head.

rience to a kid. So could a meal in a restaurant with cloth napkins and no drive-thru window. The more positive things teens are exposed to, from job choices to fine art, the broader their horizons become.

Tough Homes, Tough Cookies

Family can mean the difference between kids going to a state university or a state penitentiary, regardless of their addresses. You'll find teens from homes with a lot of good things going on, as well as bad. Remind them that, with

> Hurting kids hurt other kids.
> —*Larry Butterfield, SLAM! Youth Ministries*

God's strength, they have the power to overcome anything in their past. Let them know that Christ's forgiveness not only forgives their wrongdoings but also others' sins—especially hurtful family members'. So remain confident that good things can come from even the worst family situations. 🛑

8

Busted!

Urban youth leaders agree that one of the most frustrating aspects of youth ministry is watching their students go to jail. Sometimes it's the teen you couldn't reach. Other times, it's the teen you were about to make a leader. As disappointing as this is, just remember that good things can come out of bad circumstances like your kids going to jail—in fact, it just may be where God will reach them.

Don't Turn a Jailed Kid into a Celebrity

If a student has been in jail and returns to youth group, don't glamorize his (or her) actions. Let him know you're glad to have him back, but sadder that he had to leave. It can be good to have this teen share what happened—especially if it was a first offense—and

 The biggest disappointment is seeing youths fail in areas you hoped they would achieve in. Don't think you have failed. You only have these kids for six hours a month. Who knows where they would be if it weren't for you!
—*Esther Hall, Pathfinders International*

what he learned from it. Make a tape recording or video of that evening, and give it to the student to replay alone a year from now.

Go to Court Dates and Visitations

The same students who give you a hard time in the youth center will count the minutes 'til your first visit at jail. By all means visit your incarcerated kids (if it's allowed) and write regularly. Show up for court dates as well. It's important for these students to know you aren't giving up on them.

Teen Focus

"Jail was like college to me."

So says ChiChi, a former gangbanger from Chicago. "It was a passage of life, where the tough were expected to go." But jail is also where ChiChi finally got serious about God. ChiChi was 11 when he first heard about Christ in an urban ministries program near his home in the projects. But once his youth pastor left, it all fell apart.

"I was putting my faith in people, not God," ChiChi admits. Before long, he was involved with gangs and in and out jail for disorderly conduct and selling drugs. Once ChiChi got a gun, the offenses got more serious. ChiChi was in a paddy wagon on his way to jail when God got through to him. "If you died right now, where would you go?"

To many, it was all over for ChiChi. But he knew it was just the beginning. ChiChi used his sentence as a time to take Bible study seriously: "There are a lot of ministries in jail, with guys like me really discovering Christ for the first time." Since then ChiChi has served his sentence and is now a dynamic role model for young men in his community, teaching his crash college course, "You can be around Christ, but not involved in Christ."

Don't Let the Little Things Go Unnoticed

Once a credit card was missing from my purse. I learned it was stolen by two of my most trusted teens. I saw to it that they got more than a slap on the wrist.

Along with a serious talk with the big pastor in his office, we got these girls into a mentoring program. As expected, these mentors were needed more than my line of credit! In another incident in Chicago, a gang brawl broke out at a weekly youth event, and the police were called. As

The three scariest words I ever heard a teen utter: *Jail is fun.*
—*former youth leader, Faith Tabernacle, Chicago*

much as he hated to do it, Dana Thomas—the veteran youth pastor in the middle of the melee—decided it was best to discontinue meetings for the rest of the year. Knowing how much these teens could easily fall prey to the streets without the meetings to attend, Dana questioned his decision for months. He had no idea until years later that this incident impacted several of the kids' lives —and positively. Losing their youth center privileges caused a few teens to get on the right track with Christ and eventually enter ministry.

These kids don't have disposable income, just disposable lives.
—*youth leader, St. Louis*

The bottom line is, don't let the little things slide. Who knows what they'll turn into?

Tip: Deglamorize Jail with the Toilet Sandwich

Juan, a former teen inmate, took the cool factor away from a jail sentence by talking to his youth group about this hot treat. According to

Once a teen points out the steps outside the church where his brother was shot to death, you see that kid's dying brother every time you drop that kid off at church.
—*SLAM! youth leader, Chicago*

Juan, a toilet sandwich is just one of the culinary delights teens can look forward if they continue on their path toward prison life.

Since jail cells don't have stoves or microwaves, Juan would turn his toilet into a makeshift grill. He saved the milk cartons from his penitentiary lunch to use as

Leader Focus
After-Care Ministries

"It's easier to reach a kid in jail than in a junior high ministry," comments Scott Larson of Straight Ahead Ministries in Massachusetts. "The real challenge is when they get out. That's why after-care ministries are so important."

Located in more than 100 cities, Straight Ahead looks after young offenders once they get out of jail, prison, or juvenile homes. Larson got involved in Straight Ahead after noticing strong leadership qualities in incarcerated kids. "These are the toughest kids out there, but their leadership is geared in the wrong direction." Larson's mentoring strategy involves teaching adults role modeling. Youths live with real families—they eat with them, go to church with them, and the families help get those teens on the right path.

And Larson's efforts have paid off. He's seen a teen who was convicted of murder graduate from a Christian college with dreams of practicing law. Larson prays that God will raise up more "modern-day Nicky Cruzes" through Straight Ahead and hopes to lead 100 of these kids into full-time ministry.

charcoal in his toilet. Then he used a makeshift smooth surface, such as the stainless steel wall mirror, as a griddle. Then Juan smeared the mirror with butter he purchased in the commissary. Finally, he retrieved cheese that had been staying cool in his sink. Just grill and serve! It makes that week-old burrito in you car sound quite tasty—and three months in jail anything but.

Getting kicked out of school 20 times myself helps me deal with the "Danas" of today.

—*Dana Thomas, Executive Director, Sunshine Gospel Ministries, Chicago*

Tip: What If a Cop Asks You about a Kid?

Romans 13:1 reminds us that, "Everyone must submit himself to the governing authorities, for there is no authority except that which God has established." So don't be a lawbreaker yourself! Use this opportunity, whichever way it turns out, to discuss what's going on the teen's life.

Pray Teens Do the Right Thing— Not the Easy Thing

Imagine praying for a kid's court case—and not that he beats the case, but that he has the strength to tell the truth. That's the story of Frankie, a 14-year-old whose lawyer said he "could beat his case" but never counseled Frankie to tell the truth. When Frankie told the judge of the prayer

A house-arrest bracelet is not a fashion statement.

—*Juan, house-arrest teen, Chicago*

request that he'd have the strength to tell the truth, the judge was so stunned that he chose to try Frankie as a juvenile, not as an adult.

Telling the truth kept Frankie from serving a 20-year sentence. It just goes to show that the only way to "beat a case" is to tell the truth. It really will set you free—one way or another.

Beware the Latitude You Allow

In one incident, a student was caught using a youth center's computer equipment to download pornography. In another incident, some kids were discovered using a youth center office scanner to make counterfeit $20 bills. In both cases, the guilty parties were teens whom youth leaders trusted to work alone in the youth center! The moral of this immoral story is to make sure your youth center is a place where students go to stay out of trouble—not get into it.

> No one has done so much bad that God can't forgive, that God won't love. Being "good" won't get you into heaven.
> —*Jeff Niven, The Other Way Community Ministry, Grand Rapids, Michigan*

We need to view juvenile detention centers as ministry opportunities! And as it turns out, our involvement is a biblical mandate: "...I was in prison, and you came to visit me" (Matthew 25:36).

If there's a juvenile detention center near you (in my case, it's about 15 blocks away), I encourage you to develop a relationship with the chaplain there and consider a ministry partnership. Working with imprisoned teens will give you uncommon depth as a youth worker.

—*Efrem Smith*

USEFUL DEFINITIONS

Juvenile Court–a court system for offenders under the age of 18. But under-18 offenders can still be tried as adults.

Juvenile Detention Center–a correctional facility for under-18 offenders. This isn't a play prison by any means. JDC can be as rough as a state penitentiary.

Prison (a.k.a. the big house, state penitentiary)–home for those convicted of major offenses or felonies.

Jail–a holding bin for those awaiting trial or who have been convicted of minor offenses.

Parole–an early release from prison on the condition of good behavior.

Probation–a suspended sentence for someone convicted of a crime on the condition of good behavior. It requires reporting to a probation officer on a regular basis.

House Arrest–an alternative to jail; the offender wears an electronically monitored, irremovable ankle bracelet that notifies authorities if the offender leaves home.

Dropping Flags–giving up gang loyalty while incarcerated; often this results in severe beatings.

Rite of Passage–what many urban young men consider incarceration.

Though Jesus Forgives Teens' Pasts, the Government Does Not

One mistake can haunt some teens for the rest of their lives. With a felony charge, a teenager can rule out getting certain kinds of jobs, as well as the right to vote. In some states even first-time offenders can lose their right to vote forever. A previous record can turn even something as minor as a speeding ticket into a major fiasco. People will treat ex-con teenagers differently. But don't devote your life to finding them good lawyers or funding to beat their cases. Be a friend, a counselor—but not an enabler. You don't want to teach them to "beat the system" but to get on the right path. 🛑

9

Beat the Street

You'll never get over the shock of knowing a 10-year-old who can load an automatic weapon. Urban kids get their education on the streets. Many are in gangs or just hang with the gangs. Others are on the streets because they're runaways or throwaways. Then there are those who let the

 The upside to seeing those teens who've ditched your program to sell dope on the street corner? They see you, too!
—*Dana Thomas, Sunshine Gospel Ministries, Chicago*

street get the best of them, and they're left with a bad drug habit or worse. But even when kids fall to the pressures of the street, they're not lost. Here's how you can help...

Gangs: Membership Has Its Privileges

As weird as it might sound, many believe gangs aren't the problem, but actually a twisted solution that provides a structured group kids can belong to. Unfortunately the code of conduct for a gang isn't the same as for Boy Scouts. Once you're in a

 The strength of these kids is also their downfall. They haven't learned fear.
—*Don Stubbs, Inner City Impact, Chicago*

These kids have one of two futures: end up in prison or get killed on the streets. They don't have anyone teaching them to swim, to avoid the rough waters.
—*"Larry the White Guy," youth director, Chicago*

gang, you're in for life, which, according to statistics, will last until your early 20s. If teens don't belong to gangs, they'll hang with a gang. What's the difference? Well, if you're just hanging, you can deal drugs, shoot guns, steal cars—all without getting beaten to a pulp by your gangbanging buddies (the initiation). Now that's a deal.

Tips on Dealing with Gangs

- Remember God loves gangbangers, too, and looks at their sins the same way he looks at everybody else's sins.
- Deal with gangbanging teens as individuals, not according to their gang colors.
- Keep in mind that when gang life is all you know, it's hard to step away from it. Usually it takes tragic incidents for gang members to open up to Christ. When they get to that point, that's when to tell them they can't serve both God and their gangs.

USEFUL TERMS

Runaway–anyone under the age of 18 who's left home without permission of a parent or legal guardian.

Throwaways–anyone under the age of 18 who's been locked out or kicked out of home.

Squatters–anyone who no longer lives at home, and instead lives on a friend's couch (or a friend of a friend of a friend's couch).

Where the Girls Are–white females make up the majority of runaways, even leaving two-parent homes due to family conflicts.

- If they're serious about getting out of their gangs, they'll most likely have to move out of town and live with relatives. You might even lose contact with them. But that's better than getting killed.
- According to one study, 98 percent of gang members are dead, in prison, or maimed for life by the age of 21. The real task is getting teens to detour the gang scene in the first place. And this decision starts young. Work hand-in-hand with children's ministries to help youngsters follow Christ, not a gang lord.

Make your youth group a counter-cultural community for all youth. In other words, when kids come into your youth group, they should know that the rules are different—that in your youth group, everyone is equal. No individual or group should feel singled out as either above or below others in terms of their lifestyles outside the group. You could say something like, "In this community, things are different. The language is different, how we treat each other is different, and the love for each other is different." You can start a radical youth revolution that becomes more powerful and meaningful than any street gang! (At the same time, however, don't try to compete with street gangs, especially if you don't know much about street-gang culture.)

—*Efrem Smith*

No one can serve two masters. Either he will hate the one and love the other, or he will be devoted to the one and despise the other. You cannot serve both God and money.
—Matthew 6:24

When the Street Is Your Church

Many urban youth ministries deal primarily with homeless and run-away teens. Sad to say, homeless shelters for teens are not a government priority. Even in cities like San Francisco, it's easier to get

> If you think the school lunch is bad, try eating out of a trash can.
> —*Caleb, teen runaway*

into a trendy restaurant than to get into a shelter with an empty bed. So where do all these teens go? Like everywhere else, teens want to be with other teens. Usually there's a hot spot in the city where they all hang. So if helping homeless teens is where your heart is, if you find one street teen, you'll find more.

Whatever It Takes

If you view the street as a church without walls, a good ministry tool can be clean socks. Handing them out to homeless teens shows them love in a way a religious tract can't. John Green of Emmaus Ministries works with young men who've taken up prostitution to support their drug habits.

> The key isn't telling people about Jesus, it's people hearing about Jesus.
> —*John Green, Emmaus Ministries, Chicago*

(It's hard to find young teens hustling because "sugar daddies" gobble them up right away.) Streetwalkers are society's castaways, and more than anything else, they just want to be heard. So whether it's giving them your clothes or your listening ear, let your actions speak. It lets these kids know they're valuable in your eyes—as well as in God's eyes.

> *Fact: While most runaways return to their homes or legal guardians, about five percent make the streets their permanent address.*

Come to Me, and I Will Give You Rest

While working with street teens in Russia, leaders of Pathfinders International couldn't figure out why they kept falling asleep during the Bible study. It turns out these homeless kids were up all night being chased by the police! Since the Bible study provided their basic need for a safe place to crash, these youths experienced a very literal interpretation of Matthew 11:28. So if you find tired-eyed kids at your youth center, you may want to let them sleep. Be sure to ask them when they wake up if everything's okay.

> The toughest part about living in this neighborhood is watching the boys whose diapers you changed grow up and shoot each other.
> —*Mrs. Rodriguez, inner-city parent*

Down and Out University

When Keith Wasserman took a crash course in homelessness, it was at a school with no dorms. That's because Keith spent a few days as a homeless person on the streets. "When Jesus entered our world, he was one of us. If we're going to minister to the homeless, we should enter their world as equals." Keith, one of the founders of Good Works, Inc., can teach us a lot about dealing with homeless teens. He first gets them to begin defining themselves as God does, not as the world does. Living on the streets made Keith appreciate things such as using a clean washroom without getting hostile looks.

> Ever try to get an ID for a kid with no address?
> —*Jeff Neven, The Other Way Community Ministry, Grand Rapids, Michigan*

A drop-in center for homeless teens can be as basic as providing a safe place to hang that smells better than your average subway stop.

> *Woe to those who are heroes at drinking wine and champions at mixing drinks, who acquit the guilty for a bribe, but deny justice to the innocent.*
>
> —Isaiah 5:22-23

Users and Abusers

Sooner or later in urban youth ministry, you'll get a kid with a real drug problem. This kid knows he has problems and even wants your help. There are a lot of detox clinics hooked up to churches as well as hospitals, but you better R.S.V.P. They fill up fast, and many have long waiting lists. And once you jump through the hoops of finding an opening, don't put yourself through all those hoops again. Keep a notebook with the names of all the clinics, just in case you have to use one again.

HIV Testing

With drug activity or street hustling comes the risk of HIV. Again, know where the clinics are that test for the disease. You don't have to do everything—you just have to know where everything is. Teens who've gone to these clinics say the worst part is waiting for the results. Remember, these clinics are there to help young teens, not to condemn them during a time of crisis.

One Decision Away...

Many teenagers are only one decision away from making a life-changing mistake with unfathomable consequences. Some have

STREET SMART STORIES

The Good Samaritan: Luke 10:30-37
The Prodigal Son: Luke 15: 11-31

already made that decision. They end up on the streets, in gangs, or hustling to support their drug habits. Even if these young people don't have parents, clean clothes, or new shoes, they can have hope if you give them the gospel. And it starts by bringing Christ into their world, no matter how repulsive that world is to you. 🛑

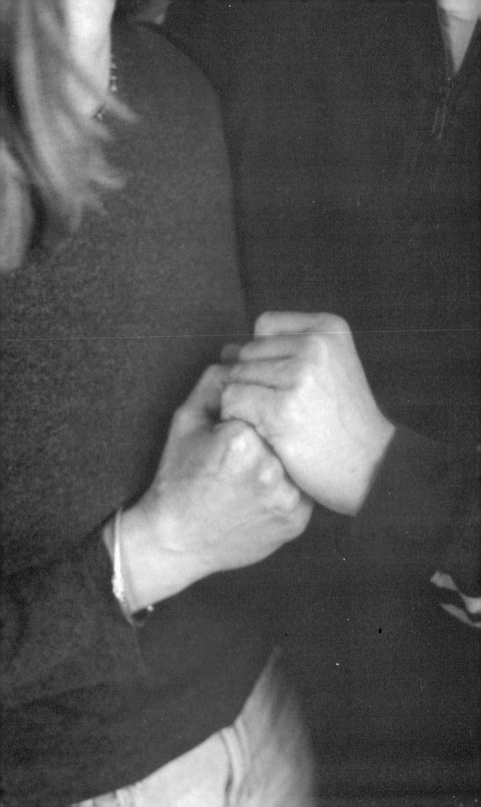

The People Who Brought You this Book...
invite you to discover MORE valuable youth ministry resources.

Youth Specialities has three decades of experience working alongside Christian youth workers of just about every denomination and youth-serving organization. We're here to help you, whether you're brand new to youth ministry or a veteran, whether you're a volunteer or a career youth pastor. Each year we serve over 100,000 youth workers worldwide through our training seminars, conventions, magazines, resource products, and internet Web site (www.YouthSpecialties.com).

For FREE information about ways YS can help your youth ministry, complete and return this card.

Are you: ☐ A paid youth worker ☐ A volunteer   S=480001

Name _____

Church/Org. _____

Address ☐ Church or ☐ Home _____

City _____ State _____ Zip _____

Daytime Phone Number (_____) _____

E-Mail _____

Denomination _____ Average Weekly Church Attendance _____

The People Who Brought You this Book...
invite you to discover MORE valuable youth ministry resources.

Youth Specialities has three decades of experience working alongside Christian youth workers of just about every denomination and youth-serving organization. We're here to help you, whether you're brand new to youth ministry or a veteran, whether you're a volunteer or a career youth pastor. Each year we serve over 100,000 youth workers worldwide through our training seminars, conventions, magazines, resource products, and internet Web site (www.YouthSpecialties.com).

For FREE information about ways YS can help your youth ministry, complete and return this card.

Are you: ☐ A paid youth worker ☐ A volunteer   S=480001

Name _____

Church/Org. _____

Address ☐ Church or ☐ Home _____

City _____ State _____ Zip _____

Daytime Phone Number (_____) _____

E-Mail _____

Denomination _____ Average Weekly Church Attendance _____

BUSINESS REPLY MAIL
FIRST-CLASS MAIL PERMIT 268 HOLMES PA

POSTAGE WILL BE PAID BY ADDRESSEE

YOUTH SPECIALTIES
P.O. BOX 668
HOLMES, PA 19043-0668

BUSINESS REPLY MAIL
FIRST-CLASS MAIL PERMIT 268 HOLMES PA

POSTAGE WILL BE PAID BY ADDRESSEE

YOUTH SPECIALTIES
P.O. BOX 668
HOLMES, PA 19043-0668

10

Gimme Some Luvin'

Save those messages about the value of your virginity for another day. To work with an urban youth group is to work with sexually active teens.

You'll have teens from long lines of single teen mothers who aren't willing to save sex for marriages that won't happen. (My personal eye-opening experience was going to a shower for a

Here are four words for ya: no wed, no bed.
—*LaTonja Horton,*
Young Life, Toledo, Ohio

former youth group member and being the only one there without a child and with a husband!)

Other teenagers are totally tuned into birth control but fail to realize there's no safe sex for the heart. Sadder yet, many are biblically illiterate, with no clue that sex outside of marriage isn't spiritually or emotionally healthy.

The bottom line is that teens are looking for love and are settling for sex. So what do you do? Replace that birth control pill with a little self-control and teach teenage boys and girls the difference between sex and real love.

Don't Talk about Sex

One way to get teens to think differently about sex is to get them to imagine a world without it. Have teens imagine what the world would be like if God decided not to create sex, knowing how much trouble it would be for us.

 You know you're having an impact on kids when you're in a grocery store with your wife and kids and then one of your students recognizes you and screams out, "There's that sex man!"
—*Theron Forshee, abstinence coach, the S.T.E.P. Foundation*

Along with rappers and rockers having nothing to sing about, what other changes would that mean on the dating scene? How would a girl show a guy she "really cared for him"? What things would a guy value about a girl?

Now if a guy can't think of anything special about the girl he's with, ask him why he's with her. Putting the focus on personal values rather than sex is a great back-door approach to dealing with promiscuity.

Three Cheers for Abstinence

We coach sports to help teens succeed, why not coach abstinence? That's exactly what got Theron Forshee to become our county's first abstinence coach. Theron works with the S.T.E.P. Foundation in Montgomery, Alabama, and speaks to about 300 teens a week, 80 percent of them sexually active. Along with supplying teens with hardcore facts, encouragement, and prayer, Theron helps teens think outside the bedposts.

 You might be the only men in these young ladies' lives who don't look at them as sex objects.
—*Efrem Smith*

"Let's get them to dream together, not to

leep together," he says. The goal is to set their minds on things other than sex and help them focus on their futures.

And Theron compares one's failed attempt at abstinence with failing a driver's test. He says just because kids fail once, they shouldn't give up abstinence forever. Not giving up is the only way you're going to get where you want to go.

> *Do you not know that he who unites himself with a prostitute is one with her in body? For it is said, "The two will become one flesh." But he who unites himself with the Lord is one with him in spirit.*
>
> —1 Corinthians 6:16-17

When my wife and I went through premarital counseling, the pastor who eventually married us brought up the issue of "soul ties." He took two pieces of paper, glued them together, and then ripped them apart before our eyes. We noticed that each piece of paper had some of the other paper still stuck to it. The pastor then looked at us and said, "This is what it's like when you have sex. A piece of another person joins a part of you and a piece of you joins a part of that person. God made sex so that two parts really become one." Then he looked at us and asked, "How many people have you been 'one with' before marriage? Because you carry those people into marriage."

I couldn't hold my head up because I realized right then the true meaning of keeping your virginity until marriage, and I had given up mine as a teen. Every time I share this story with youth, I'm amazed at the impact. I can't tell you that it's kept all of my students from giving away their virginity, but I can tell you that the best way to talk about sex with urban youth is to be real, to tell the truth—especially about your own life.

—*Efrem Smith*

Get Your Hands on Some Abstinence Curriculum

Schools do a pretty good job at handing out birth control, but many fail to teach about sex or the reality of the pain caused by sex before marriage.

Wait Training and *Why Am I Tempted?* are two of many abstinence curriculums or booklets you can use with your teens. Youth Specialties' Good Sex kit is an excellent source of study and information. Many public schools are open to abstinence teachers speaking to students, so that's a great way for you to reach more teens.

But like all good curriculum, you have to spend time learning the material.

Many programs like *Wait Training* require you to become a certified teacher of the material. But the teens are worth the investment.

BEEN THERE, DONE IT

What if your students ask you about your sexual past? If answering truthfully can keep them from making the same mistake, go for it. But if they're just asking to ask, move on. Be truthful, but tasteful. Use your common sense. Don't belittle the pain your mistakes caused you.

Shower or No Shower?

A teenage girl in your youth group gets pregnant (the wrong thing), but doesn't have an abortion (the right thing). What do you do? Do you honor her with a fancy shower or do you shun her?

 Okay, so why did God give us bodies that say yes and a Bible that says no?

—*Ferrari, age 15, Chicago*

If a girl does get pregnant, you're going to want to help supply this young mom what she needs. God calls the church to do that (James 1:27), along with visiting orphans and widows in their distress. If you choose to have a get-together, use this time to tell her and her friends about the rough road ahead, how life as a single teen mom will be "no party." Use this opportunity to let her to talk from her heart and share her fears, as well as to pray for her and her baby.

Pro-Love

There's nothing positive about abortion. But sometimes we make the mistake of aborting the mother. Her sin becomes unforgivable, and her heartaches become unimportant. Remember God promises to forgive us if we repent. But we have to help these young women forgive themselves, too.

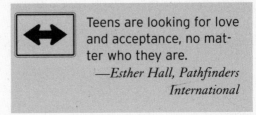

Teens are looking for love and acceptance, no matter who they are.
—*Esther Hall, Pathfinders International*

Your job as a youth leader is to keep teenage girls from ever having to make the decision between pregnancy and abortion. Most important, make sure you demonstrate unconditional love for them, regardless of what they choose.

How to Hang Up on a Booty Call

Phil Jackson might share his name with a famous basketball coach, but you'll never confuse the two. This Phil is president of 911 Urban Youth Ministries as well as the youth pastor at Lawndale Community Church, where he brings together the knockout combination of creativity and guts.

One issue that Phil is passionate about is valuing yourself and your body. He usually starts with the analogy of going into a jewelry store where someone has changed all the price tags. Items that were worth a lot are now seemingly valueless. "That's what's happened with sex. Teens have forgotten its value."

According to Phil, you want to challenge young men to be men. You want to push that ego button by reminding them that "they're the men!" and telling them they shouldn't let their bodies decide what decisions they'll make. Even more, they shouldn't let women have that kind of control over them, he says. For the girls, Phil reminds them that they're worth the wait.

Most important, Phil says, "You want to have groups where girls are accountable to each other, learning what it is to be ladies, and young men raise the bar for each other." He also discusses with each group their plans for the future, and how having a baby would jack up those plans. He also gets teens to talk about the pain in their lives caused by not knowing their father or having a relationship with him.

Teen Focus
Gung Ho about Saying No

Shawntel is just like any other 15-year-old girl from the city—until she opens her mouth. That's because Shawntel is surprisingly vocal about being pro-life and has no problem telling the boys to keep their hands to themselves. Why such strong convictions from such a young girl? Well, Shawntel's mother was a teen mom, and so was her grandmother, and Shawntel does not want to continue the cycle. (Actually, Shawntel's family tree is six generations deep with 15-year-old single moms.)

Shawntel's story takes another twist when she describes her mother's pregnancy with her. Her mother was at an abortion clinic when a woman passed her a pamphlet that made her change her mind. Shawntel is mighty thankful for that lady! Now with God's help, Shawntel is determined to be the first 15-year-old in her family that doesn't get pregnant.

Did You Jack Up Somebody's Plans?

Get teens to go back to the goal-setting exercise—but have them map out their parents' goals this time. Have them compare the connection between their moms' and dads' unfulfilled dreams and their own full diapers. They will see how they—as bouncing babies—actually bounced them off track from nursing school, beauty college, or some other goal.

Keep Their Eyes Open

Here's a wake-up call for the ladies. Next time you're at the mall, have them count how many teen moms they see pushing baby strollers. Then have them count how many teen guys they see doing the same. It's a great way for girls to open their eyes to who's out the door once that baby comes into the world.

Put Your Soul into It

Here's a funky lesson that gets teens to think differently about sex. All you need are some old Nikes and a Visa card. Pull out your credit card, and tell your students you'll buy them any pair of new shoes they want. Let them cry out responses: "Nikes!" "Adidas!" Then ask who would want an old pair you brought. Few would want used merchandise. Ask them why they're more concerned about where they put their feet than where they put their hearts, which are far more precious.

Foot powder can cure whatever disease you get from a shoe. But that's not true for things you can catch from being careless with our hearts. Remind teens that unless they want to become used merchandise—and less desirable than someone else's funky old sneakers—they should keep their hands and other body parts to themselves. Be sure to emphasize that Christ's forgiveness can make all of us like new, regardless of our pasts.

Set Guidelines for Those Who Can't

The best way to keep your pants on is to stay in places where you can't take them off. Create a checklist for your girls and guys, making them tune in to what turns them on. Then challenge them to avoid those situations.

Okay. God made you human, which means certain things will get your hormones buzzin'. What things turn your bodies on and your brains off?

_____ hot and heavy kissing

_____ fondling of anything

_____ being anywhere together alone

_____ things she (or he) wears

_____ having birth control

_____ using drugs or drinking

_____ certain TV shows and music videos

_____ having had sex before

_____ knowing that she (he) is willing

_____ certain things she (he) says

_____ certain things you say

_____ wanting to brag about it to your friends

_____ being afraid your friends will find out you didn't do it

_____ believing sex is what makes you a man (or popular with the guys)

_____ believing sex is no big deal

Speaking of Forgiveness

When you talk openly about love and sex with urban youth, be as prepared to deal as much with forgiveness as you are about sexually transmitted diseases (STDs). Many of your teens are sexually active—some have had abortions, others were responsible for them, some have STDs, others are victims of incest. Emphasize that no matter what's in their pasts, God can forgive them completely, even when they have a hard time forgiving themselves. Also remind them of the importance of forgiving others, and that God offers the only kind of love that will satisfy them forever.

Gimme a Little TLC

It's easy to focus on promiscuity, making it the sin of all sins. By doing so, you just might make teens think about it more, rather than less. So it's time to learn a lesson from Christ.

Jesus didn't lose his cool with the sinful women or prostitutes. Instead he gave these women the unconditional love and forgiveness

> Your best abstinence program is really not talking about sex so much as it's talking about the sexes.
> —*Phil Jackson, Lawndale Community Church, Chicago*

they craved. Teens need your love and acceptance, regardless of the decisions they make. So constantly remind the young ladies (and do call them young ladies) that they are worth the wait, and that they should focus on their talents and abilities. Equally as important is raising the bar for young men (and do call them young men or gentlemen) to be true leaders.

And never forget, the real issue isn't sex. It's all about love. 🛑

11

All Rapped Up

C an the explicit lyrics of this generation compare to the explicit lyrics of yours? While many dangers are unique to their urban environment, one of the biggest dangers facing urban teens is the media itself. Today's marketers "coolhunt" urban areas for the next fashion and music trends, turning urban youth into prime-time role models for teens everywhere. Not only does the media create an insatiable appetite for wants, it glamorizes all the things you try to keep teenagers from doing. But

 The biggest danger to urban teens isn't gangs or guns or drugs. It's the media. The television screen gives kids an appetite for more of what they're already watching.
—*Dana Thomas, Sunshine Gospel Ministries, Chicago*

warning your kids about what they should and shouldn't listen to and watch will do as much good as when your youth leaders warned you!

But there is a way to get everything—from the TV to designer labels—to actually work in your favor. Here are some tips to get all that media input to improve your output.

Tune into the Psalms

If you can't stop teens from listening to gangsta rap, at least use it to get them to read lyrics from the original rapper, David. Ask teens to bring in their favorite CDs and read the lyrics off of the labels. Compare them to the words of the Psalms. How are they alike? How are they different? How does David deal with vengeance, enemies, and anger differently than today's rappers?

The Joy of Cola versus the Joy of Jesus

Why is it that teens seem to know every word from their favorite pop commercials, but it's like pulling teeth to get them to sing about Jesus? Why not try a lesson in which you have them recall their favorite commercial jingles or TV show theme songs? Then ask them what good it will do them to sing about soft drinks when they need a little courage. (You can also have them sing their favorite G-rated hit single.) Use this illustration to focus on the importance of memorizing Scripture.

Warning Labels: What Do Your Ears Taste?

To be a teenager is to be an eating machine. But your mouth isn't the only thing you feed. Your eyes, your curiosity, your ears are always absorbing information. Try to get your students to examine what they're feeding their ears for once.

Bring a box of cotton swabs to the youth group meeting and ask for volunteers to clean out their ears—and then ask them to let you have a little taste of what they've been listening to. (You have a cotton swab hidden that you have dabbed in honey or apple butter—which looks anything but tasty or sweet on the end of a cotton swab—that you can smuggle into the exercise). Take a taste. Your kids will never forget that what comes out of your ears isn't as nasty as some of those lethal lyrics that go into them.

Unplug Your Teens

If your budget isn't big enough to support multimedia presentations, count your blessings. It's easier for you to have unplugged meetings where electronic noise doesn't compete with the message. But don't stop there. Why not try a media fast? Challenge your students to go a day or week without TV or their favorite music. Come back and talk about what it was like. Was it easier to tune into God when their headphones were off?

The 17-Minute Challenge

In any given hour of TV programming, there's an average of 17 minutes of commercials. Why not challenge teens to unplug from TV for that amount of time each day and plug into God? You'll find it's something easy for

 TV is a curse. It's the electronic church. Kids are learning how to live through TV.
—*Danny Lopez, youth pastor, Chicago*

teens to remember, since they'll be reminded of this challenge every time their favorite show has a commercial break! Plugging into prayer, Bible study, and personal worship for 17 minutes a day will keep kids tuned into God in the long run.

Image Is Everything

Designer labels and name brands are as important to urban teenagers as they are to every other kid. While it's important for them to feel good about themselves, it's also important for urban teens to know that the best thing about them isn't what they wear, but their inner qualities designed by God. Bring in your old yearbooks and let your students try to guess who was popular and who was not just based on the dated wardrobes. Then do a talk about the only designer outfit worth putting on—the Armor of God (Ephesians 6:10-17).

Wanna Be a Cover Girl?

A fun all-night activity for girls is a night of real beauty makeovers. While they get out the hair spray, nail polish, and hair extensions, use this as an opportunity to talk about real beauty (1 Peter 3:3-4).

Some girls might need tips on toning down their looks or dress, and others might need help feeling prettier. If you know of anyone in your church that works as a makeup artist or hairdresser or is in the clothing business, bring her along for expert tips. Best of all, you can use this girls-only time to talk about the godly beauty that doesn't fade away with age.

Zap the Insta-Christian Concept

One of the dangers of living in a society filled with convenience products is that teens are more likely to believe that being a Christian is just as effortless. Let them know that there's no such thing as an insta-Christian. For an illustration, check out the ingredients of their favorite instant product. Notice how many are fake or artificial. Then point out that to be an insta-Christian is to be a fake. Being real takes time and effort.

Beeper for Jesus

If you want to get urban teens to listen to you, don't try talking to them…beep 'em! Use this analogy to get them talking to God. How many times a day is God trying to talk to you, but you're tuning out his voice? Would you be more willing to listen to God if he supplied you with a spiritual beeper or if you met him in a chat room? Draw the conclusion that talking to God is as easy as talking to anybody else—and there are no roaming charges. (If you have a beeper, have someone page you at an appropriate time during your talk to make your kids think for a moment that it's coming from heaven's hotline.)

We must provide youth with cutting-edge Christian rap and hip-hop. Most of us don't have 24-hour contemporary Christian radio stations. And most Christian bookstores aren't very "urban teen friendly"—or they're far away. So the only way our kids can hear about groups such as L.A. Symphony, the Cross Movement, G.R.I.T.S., Tonex, and others is if we spread the word. Try throwing a Christian hip-hop house party or challenge your students to turn over to you their mainstream rap CDs that contain negative messages—and then you can replace them with Christian rap CDs.

But whatever you do, please don't give sub-par Christian rap to your kids! That's like replacing Pepsi with prune juice—ya know what I'm sayin'? Try contacting Christian record labels, too, and share your vision for how their music can impact the lives of urban youth—many labels are more than happy to get music into kids' hands as a promotional tool. (And you get free tunes!)

—*Efrem Smith*

Inquiring Minds Want to Know

If you want to get a clearer picture of who your teens really are, why not let them show you? Have them bring in their favorite magazines (or see if you can get some for free from a beauty salon). Ask them to cut out pictures that remind them of some aspect of themselves. You'll be surprised at how much those pictures reflect! But don't stop there. Ask all your students if a cover story were written about them, what would it say?

Know What They're Plugged Into

Coming from the world of advertising, I know that in an average year, a teens is exposed to 750,000 messages on TV, radio, the Internet, billboards, and magazines. And that's a conservative estimate. That doesn't even count the number of messages conveyed by way of other music sources, movies, and other printed media. But even with all those messages competing for your students' attention, there's only one that really matters—the message of Christ.

Urban youth face a lot of unique challenges, but don't forget the importance of battling TV, music, and other electronic media. While you may not watch the same TV shows or listen to the same music, it's important to know what your teens are plugged into and why. Songs and videos might not give you insights into what's happening outside a teen's window, but they can give you peaks at what's going on inside their minds and hearts. And that's the biggest battleground of all. ⬤

12

Word!

Believe it or not, one of the goals of urban youth ministry is to teach the Bible. But how do you make that burgundy, leather-bound book pertinent to today's city-dwelling kids? First, take the time to assess where your students are spiritually and what lessons they need most—chances are it's not an in-depth study of Obadiah.

A good place to start is with stories that could come right from the newspaper headlines: convicts, teen mothers, poverty, and racism. Here are some favorite lessons from urban youth leaders around the country:

 These teens are suffering from biblical illiteracy. They haven't read the stories of Jonah or Job, nor have they heard of them. If Hollywood didn't make a movie about it, they don't know about it.
—*Don Stubbs, Inner City Impact, Chicago*

Esther: A Big-Time Minority

Not only was Esther a minority, but also she was in a country that didn't like her race. Plus, Esther was a foster kid to her Uncle Mordecai because both her parents were dead (Esther 2:7). But Esther didn't let these obstacles stop her from being everything God wanted her to be. And one day, she became a queen. ("Esther," by the way, is Persian for "star.")

Application: Ask your students how their ethnicity, neighborhood, and home situations can bring them closer to God? How are they "stars" in God's eyes?

Real Turf Wars

If you think turf wars started with gangbanging, think again. Joshua and his men killed thousands at a time. And they weren't battling over drug territory. There was something much sweeter at stake—the land of milk and honey. But the big difference between what Joshua did and what's being done on the streets is that God planned Joshua's battles.

Application: One thing teens can learn from Joshua is the importance of godly courage at all times, including the courage to resist gang pressures. Viewing the battles of Joshua as "turf wars" can put a new twist on Old Testament history. Key Verse: "Have I not commanded you? Be strong and of courage; do not be terrified; do not be discouraged, for the Lord your God is with you where you go" (Joshua 1:9).

Another Brother

Joseph had the wardrobe, the looks—and the chance for a little action with his master's wife. But Joseph refused her come ons and split the scene. She even ripped his coat in the process. Why did Joseph refuse such an opportunity? Because he knew that fooling around with his master's wife would be wrong in God's eyes no matter how good it might feel. While Joseph suffered some immediate consequences for his upright decision, in the long run he

> ⬌ If you're looking for a young man who decided to not compromise his relationship with God, look at Joseph.
> —*Dana Thomas, Sunshine Gospel Ministries, Chicago*

prospered, saving Egypt from destruction and gaining favor with its people, most notably Pharaoh.

Application: Joseph is a great example of a man who said no to sex outside of marriage in the face of incredible temptation. It is possible to do! Make the point that Joseph was smart to flee the scene and not put himself in a tempting situation (Genesis 39:2-23; 2 Timothy 2:22).

From Convict to Convicted

Think God only uses people with perfect pasts? Think again. Some of God's biggest winners started out as big-time losers, such as Moses and Paul. Moses was wanted for murder, and Paul killed Christians for a living. And while they both were convicted of murder, they both turned from their previous lifestyles and got right with God (Exodus 2-3; Acts 9:1-22).

Paul did time and still did a lot for the Lord. No one is too bad to end up good.
—*William T. Sherrod, SLAM! Youth Ministries, Chicago*

Application: Moses and Paul are two great examples of why teens shouldn't let anything from their pasts stop them from doing what's right today. Remind them how important it is to turn from their previous lifestyles completely, not just on Sundays.

Squabbling Sistas

Mary and Martha were two sisters who did what sisters do best. Fight. They even had a bit of a blowout in front of Jesus! While Martha was busy doing chores, Mary was visiting with the Son of God. This made Martha lose her cool. She complained to Jesus that her sister wasn't helping her. But Jesus chided Martha, saying that Mary's concerns were far more important than housework (Luke 10:38-42).

Application: This is a great story that illustrates the complexities of sibling altercations. While God may have made you and your sibling different, God loves you both the same. Ask your kids with brothers and sisters what they "fight" about at home. Are they big things or little things? What can they do to curb the knockdown, drag-outs?

Fat Cats and Hot Nights

Daniel is a great example of what God can do with a courageous teen. First, Daniel didn't give into the tempting foods and feasts offered by the king at "Club Neb" (a.k.a. the table of King Nebuchadnezzar) in Daniel 1:8. Daniel and his friends didn't cave under peer pressure and bow down to King Nebuchadnezzar, either. That's how Daniel and his friends, Shadrach, Meshach, and Abednego, ended up spending a heated night in a fiery furnace.

No one has done too much bad for God to forgive him, for God to love him. It's not how good you are, but your faith that gets you into heaven.

—*Jeff Neven, The Other Way Community Ministry, Grand Rapids, Michigan*

Application: Daniel is the ultimate example of how God can use teens for important tasks. Daniel honored God by what he chose to eat and drink at a party, as well as by not bowing down to idols. Ask teens, what hot situations have they encountered because they stuck by their beliefs? Would they be willing to bypass beer at a party to honor God?

The Leader Formally Known as Prince

Moses was an abandoned baby who ended up with a lifestyle of the rich and famous. Although he grew up in a palace as the adopted son of the Pharaoh's daughter, his real desire was to help his people—the Jewish people. So Moses gave up his fancy digs in order to lead the Jewish slaves out of Egypt and be faithful to God (Exodus 2).

Application: Moses is an excellent example of someone who placed no importance on material things. Ask your teens *how important is it that they live in fancy homes? Will that make them happy? Did it make Moses happy?* Let teens understand while nice things are fine to have, they aren't everything.

What Are You Waiting for? Christmas?

Mary and Joseph were two teenagers in love. Even though they were well on their way toward marriage, they decided to wait for sex. Good thing they did. If Mary had messed around just once, she would have blown God's plan for her to be Jesus's virgin mother (Luke 2:1-7).

Application: This is an effective example of the importance of self-control. If these two teens could wait, anyone can. Ask your young ladies if God wanted to choose a teenage girl today to be the mother of Jesus, would he be able to find someone? What would her friends think of a modern-day Mary? But don't stop there. Ask your young men if they have what it takes to be a Joseph? Would they have that kind of self-control, even if they were engaged?

Use this story to let teens know that having sex now can do more than mess up their lives; it can mess up bigger plans God has in mind.

> Don't go into urban youth ministry to convert the culture—the music, the food, the styles, the language. Embrace the differences. How do you reach God in their "world"?
> —*urban youth pastor, Memphis*

The Book of Answers to Life's Big Questions

Your most important task is to make the Bible relevant to these teens' lives. Almost any verse from Proverbs can help teens avoid the school of hard knocks. The first few chapters are great for those involved in gangbanging and street violence. Another good lesson is to have teens imagine that there's a book in the Bible named after them—and what would be the main story? Would they be portrayed like Moses or Judas?

 As a teen, I knew more than anybody else in the world. It took a few more years to realize I didn't know jack.
—*22-year-old, Chicago*

Remember the Bible can be viewed as a book full of stories about old men who hang out with sheep or full of stories about people no different than us. So keep your teens in mind when you plan your their lessons. Word! 🛑

13

911 Verses

eed verses for emergency situations? Check these out:

Be Nice to Cops

Submit yourselves for the Lord's sake to every authority instituted among men: whether to the king, as the supreme authority, or to governors, who are sent by him to punish those who do wrong and to commend those who do right.

—1 Peter 2:13-14

1-800-Call-and-Get-Saved

...call upon me in the day of trouble; I will deliver you, and you will honor me.

—Psalm 50:15

Silence the Violence

...I take no pleasure in the death of the wicked, but rather that they turn from their ways and live. Turn! Turn from your evil ways!

—Ezekiel 33:11

Reconsider Your Friends

Do not be mislead: "Bad company corrupts good character."

—1 Corinthians 15:33

Think This Over Before You Think about Gettin' Jiggy wit It

It is God's will that you should be sanctified: that you should avoid sexual immorality; that each of you should learn to control his own body in a way that is holy and honorable, not in passionate lust like the heathen, who do not know God.

—1 Thessalonians 4:3-5

Money Ain't the Answer

Whoever loves money never has money enough; whoever loves wealth is never satisfied with his income.

—Ecclesiastes 5:10

Erase Racism

If anyone says, "I love God," yet hates his brother, he is a liar. For anyone who does not love his brother, whom he has seen, cannot love God, whom he has not seen.

—1 John 4:20

Just Say No to "Yo Momma!" Jokes

Do not let any unwholesome talk come out of your mouths, but only what is helpful for building others up according to their needs, that it may benefit those who listen.

—Ephesians 4:29

Forget about Taking the "Five Finger Discount"

He who has been stealing must steal no longer, but must work, doing something useful with his own hands, that he may have something to share with those in need.

—Ephesians 4:28

Pray for Those Who Talk Behind Your Back

But I tell you: love your enemies and pray for those who persecute you.

—Matthew 5:44

SLAM! Youth Ministries in Chicago divided verses into six teen-friendly categories: *You, Who, True, Guts, Buts,* and *Now What?*

You

You are a winner.

If you want to see a real winner, you don't have to look at a box of Wheaties. Just look in the mirror. God put as much time into making you as he did Michael Jordan.

For you created my inmost being; you knit me together in my mother's womb. I praise you because I am fearfully and wonderfully made; your works are wonderful, I know that full well.

—Psalm 139:13-14

You are deeper than your skin.

What can you tell about a person based on her skin color?
Uhh…nothing. But hating people because of their skin color says a lot

about you.

Anyone who claims to be in the light but hates his brother is still in the darkness.

—1 John 2:9

You've got the right stuff.

It doesn't matter if you don't look like a supermodel or dress one like either. It's what's inside that counts.

Your beauty should not come from adornment, such as braided hair and wearing of gold jewelry and fine clothes. Instead, it should be that of your inner self, the unfading beauty of a gentle and quiet spirit, which is of great worth in God's sight.

—1 Peter 3:3-4

You and your attitude.

If you have a bad one, you'd better change it. Having a positive attitude is the first step to changing your future.

Do everything without complaining or arguing, so that you may be blameless and pure, children of God without fault in a crooked and depraved generation, in which you shine like stars in the universe.

—Philippians 2:14-15

Who

Who's your family?

No matter how messed up your family is, you've been adopted into a good one.

[In love] he predestined us to be adopted as his sons through Jesus Christ, in accordance with his pleasure and will...

—Ephesians 1:5

Who's acting like a child?

Sometimes parents can act like children or worse. Sometimes they hurt us, abandon us, and do things that are far from loving. Remember these things are not your fault. This is not what your heavenly father intended.

...you are the helper of the fatherless.

—Psalm 10:14

Who's your hero?

Just whom do you worship? Is it a rapper? Your older brother? If whomever you worship doesn't worship Christ, you have a problem.

Do not envy wicked men, do not desire their company; for their hearts plot violence, and their lips talk about making trouble.

—Proverbs 24:1-2

Who's your church?

Who's building you up in the Word? If the church isn't setting your values, what is?

Let us not give up meeting together, as some are in the habit of doing, but let us encourage one another—and all the more as you see the Day approaching.

—Hebrews 10:25

Who got you angry?

Who did you wrong? Is it your half sister? Someone at school? Even when people mess up, it's important to make up.

"In your anger, do not sin": Do not let the sun go down while you're still angry...

—Ephesians 4:26

True

True love

What is love? Have I ever really felt it? Why does messing around sexually make me feel lonely afterwards? If you're looking for the true definition of love, don't turn to the TV, turn to these words—

Love is patient, love is kind. It does not envy, it does not boast, it is not proud. It is not rude, it is not self-seeking, it is not easily angered, it keeps no record of wrongs. Love does not delight in evil but rejoices with the truth. It always protects, always trusts, always helps, always perseveres. Love never fails.

—1 Corinthians 13:4-8

True value

Are you treating your body like second-hand merchandise? You don't let friends use your basketball shoes—make sure you don't let them use your body either.

...you were bought at a price. Therefore honor God with your body.

—1 Corinthians 6:20

Tried and true ways to wait

What's the best way to keep those pants on and stay out of trouble? Stay in places where you can't take them off!

Flee the evil desires of youth, and pursue righteousness, faith, love, and peace, along with those who call on the Lord out of a pure heart.

—2 Timothy 2:22

True forgiveness

Even if you messed up, had an abortion, were responsible for one, were the victim of incest, were sexually abused, or have a bad rep, Christ still loves you.

Therefore, if any anyone is in Christ, he is a new creation; the old has gone, the new has come!

—2 Corinthians 5:17

Guts

Guts to cry

It's normal to be afraid of some things—like drive-bys and violence. And it's okay to cry about them. But there's one thing you shouldn't be afraid of—God.

The Lord is close to the brokenhearted and saves those who are crushed in spirit.

—Psalm 34:18

Guts to stand up

If you don't have the guts to stand up to your friends, they are not your friends.

Be strong and courageous. Do not be terrified; do not be discouraged, for the LORD your God will be with you wherever you go.

—Joshua 1:9

Guts to be yourself

Are you afraid people wouldn't like you if they knew who you are inside? God wants you to have the courage to be yourself—and he can give it to you.

For God did not give us a spirit of timidity, but a spirit of power, of love, and of self-discipline.

—2 Timothy 1:7

Guts to follow Christ

Following Jesus takes more guts than joining a gang or following the crowd. Do you have what it takes to do it?

I am not ashamed of the gospel, because it is the power of God for the salvation of everyone who believes...

—Romans 1:16

When guts aren't enough

If a friend gets shot or if your mother loses her job, does that mean God doesn't love you? If things like that are tough with God on your side, just imagine how rough those things would be without him.

And we know that in all things God works for the good of those who love him, who have been called according to his purpose.

—Romans 8:28

Buts

But I'm too dumb for school...

Let us not become weary in doing good, for at the proper time we will reap a harvest if we do not give up.

—Galatians 6:9

But being bad feels so good...

Do not conform any longer to the pattern of this world, but be transformed by the renewing of your mind. Then you will be able to test and approve what God's will is—his good, pleasing and perfect will.

—Romans 12:2

But only rich people get ahead...

Commit to the LORD whatever you do, and your plans will succeed.

—Proverbs 16:3

Now What?

Now start studying it.

Don't let anyone look down on you because you are young, but set an example for the believers in speech, in life, in love, in faith and in purity.

—1 Timothy 4:12

Now walk it.

If we claim to have fellowship with him yet walk in the darkness, we lie and do not live by the truth. But if we walk in the light, as he is in the light, we have fellowship with one another, and the blood of Jesus, his Son, purifies us from all sin.

—1 John 1:6-7

Now talk it.

If you're not sharing Christ, what are you sharing? What is your tongue saying about your beliefs in God?

I pray that you may be active in sharing your faith, so that you will have a full understanding of every good thing we have in Christ.

—Philemon 1: 6

Now breathe it.

Is God as important to your everyday existence as the air you breathe? If not, why not?

So I say, live by the Spirit, and you will not gratify the desires of the sinful nature.

—Galatians 5:16

Now go for it!

What's stopping you from developing a relationship with God or chasing that dream? Nothing but yourself.

Ask and it will be given to you; seek and you will find; knock and the door will be opened to you. For everyone who asks receives; he who seeks finds; and to him that knocks, the door will be opened.

—Matthew 7:7-8 🛑

14

Goals for Down the Road

For whatever reason, the inner city isn't a place where young people set goals. Some blame it on bad schooling. Others blame it on lack of role models. But Efrem Smith, the executive director of Minneapolis' Park Avenue Foundation, sums it up best: "The reason urban teens don't make much of their lives is because they don't believe they can do it!" It's sad but true. The majority of

The mindset for some of these kids is that you aren't expected to excel. They haven't seen it done before. It's time to change that.
—*Theron Forshee, the S.T.E.P. Foundation, Montgomery, Alabama*

urban teens are running on empty when it comes to self-esteem. But as their youth leader, you have the chance to change that.

How? By helping them set short-term goals that will eventually turn into long-term ones. When you help young teens realize they're talented, creative, smart, and gifted, you can help them see the potential God gave them. But don't limit these goals and creative abilities to what teens can do at your church or youth center. You can help students realize their potential outside the youth group, too.

On Building Self-Esteem

Before you expect teenagers to go to college, you have to help them believe they can graduate the eighth grade. But before they believe they can do that, they have to believe they're smart. So make it your goal to build students' self-esteem one step at a time. Without self-esteem, they won't believe they can do anything.

How? Teach them a new skill—from how to change a tire all the way to how to ski. Equally important, teach them to not be afraid of failure. How? By letting them know about your personal failures—and what you learned from them. These could be your most embar-

Youth ministries must be ready to address the needs of the whole teenager. If you just focus on Sunday school but not the social and academic needs, you're missing the mark.

—*Efrem Smith*

rassing moments as a teen, your talent for striking out, or how you flunked your driver's test three times before passing. Finally, let your kids teach you something new, too.

Mapping out a Future

Getting kids on the right path can take little more than a blank piece of paper:

Just sit with them and write down their dreams and goals and ideal destinations. Start with the final destination (heaven) and fill in stops along the way. Ask your student where she wants to be five weeks from now. Then five years from now. Ask her what steps she's currently taking to reach

These kids have to know that they can do more than paint graffiti on walls. They can use that same talent to get a good job!

—*Glenda, inner-city public school teacher*

those goals? Be sure to concentrate on the things that she can do each week that can make her goals a reality.

Other points:

- Be sure to remind her that the toughest thing about setting any goal is writing it down on paper. Then it becomes real.
- If her goals seem high, she might not necessarily reach them, but she won't end up in the gutter, either. Just make sure she's prepared for not reaching some of her goals as well, especially if they're too high. (For instance, the chronic school skipper setting a goal to change his ways and pull straight A's...or a teen counting on being a professional athlete and nothing else.) Regardless of her dreams, help her recognize the talents God gave her to even begin striving after those goals.

"Life's a Trip! What's Your Road Map?"

When it comes to finding direction in life, the Bible is the best place to look. Not only does it communicate our worth in God's eyes, it tells us how to reach our goals. Using the analogy of the Bible as a road map is an easy way to make sure teens are on the right path, as well as assuring them that God gave them talents—and has plans to use them.

These teens are living for the moment.
—*inner-city youth leader, St. Louis*

Your word is a lamp to my feet and a light for my path.
—Psalm 119:105

Recognizing Dead Ends

Life is full of dead ends—gangs, stealing, drinking, drugs, and it's-only-wrong-if-I-get-caught sex. Though they might seem fun at the time, these dead ends will quickly put an end to a high-risk teen's dreams.

> *...open their eyes and turn them from darkness to light, and from the power of Satan to God, so that they may receive forgiveness of sins.*
>
> —Acts 26:18

Dead-End Derrick

Derrick could have been the student leader of his youth group. Lots of charisma, manners, good looks, and smarts. As much as the youth group wanted Derrick's qualities, so did the gangs. Little by little, Derrick's attitude started slipping, mouthing off to leaders as well as to his mother. He joined a gang and started living by their rules. One night, Derrick made a decision that changed his path forever. Instead of hanging around the youth center, Derrick joined his gang to beat a rival gang member with a baseball bat. That was the end of Derrick's fun. Miraculously, the victim survived with no permanent injuries. (God has mercy on rival gang members, too.) Derrick and the rest of his gang were hauled off to jail. Derrick waited for his trial for months—behind bars. There he became appreciative of the cards and visits from family and youth leaders. Though it was sad that Derrick was in jail, it turned out that God had him right where he wanted him. For the first time in months, Derrick had his Bible open—and was open to the gospel, too. Dead ends might be bad, but they might be just what a teen needs to turn to Christ.

More Urban Roadkill

Travis—a charismatic, bright teen from the south side of Chicago—looks like the all-American kid you'd see flipping burgers in a fast-food commercial. But nothing could be further from the truth. Travis couldn't tell you much about his plans for the future, but he could tell you how to load a semiautomatic weapon. Travis has been stabbed as well as shot, and he has seen people shoot up as well as shoot guns—and die alone in the street. Travis was proud to be a father, proud to be a gangbanger, and indifferent toward dropping out of school—quite a life for a sixteen-year-old.

When asked where he wanted to be five years from now, Travis answered in all seriousness, "I want to be dead." Though his answer was startling at first, Travis explained how heaven—a place filled with peace instead of drive-bys—felt like his best option.

Travis's big plan for the future was to die young.

Beware of Potholes

While dead ends are obviously detrimental to the future of urban teens, so are foul mouths and bad attitudes. These things, while seemingly minor compared to other things urban youths can get into, are potholes on their paths. Other potholes include lack of motivation and destructive habits. Whatever the potholes, they can keep teens from getting where they want to go—

Once a youth pastor, always a youth pastor. Fifteen years from now, you'll still be the youth pastor to the kids who are now the parents of kids in your youth group. It's a lifelong commitment.

—*Dana Thomas, Sunshine Gospel Ministries, Chicago*

from making the basketball team to developing a relationship with Christ. So evaluate the potholes in your students' lives and repair them right away. Scripture has some effective remedies:

Hit a Pothole?	Repair It with...
Lack of self-esteem	*Philippians 4:13*
Lack of motivation	*Proverbs 10:26; 19:15*
Bad attitude	*Philippians 2:14-16*
Swearing	*Proverbs 17:20*
Cheating	*Proverbs 10:2-11*

What Larry Says

Larry—a veteran urban youth worker for more than a quarter century—knows the importance of setting goals for teens. He has used the map analogy for years, helping teens get back on the right path. "The Bible is a good map to help anyone get where he or she wants to go, whether it's you making inroads in urban ministry or

Don't look at who a teen is now, but rather where he'll be five years down the road.
—*Larry Butterfield, SLAM! Youth Ministries, Chicago*

a teen making his way out of jail." Larry also warns us to focus on who your students will be in the future, not just their current states. "If you see big dead ends in the future, work with that student. If there are only a few trouble zones that kid has to detour now, hang tight."

But Larry's most important advice is to have fun doing it. Teens will mirror your attitude. If you feel defeated, so will they.

So make it your goal to help your kids set a few goals of their own. Keep them pumped on Scripture as well. That way they'll have godly esteem in their tank to get them where they want to go.

More Esteem-Building Verses

*The LORD will fulfill [his purpose] for me; your love, O
LORD, endures forever— do not abandon the works of your
hands.*

—Psalm 138:8

*That is why, for Christ's sake, I delight in weaknesses, in insults,
in hardships, in persecutions, in difficulties. For when I am
weak, then I am strong.*

—2 Corinthians 12:10

Your Goals Aren't Crazy!

*Delight yourself in the LORD and he will give you the desires
of your heart.*

—Psalm 37:4

*"For I know the plans I have for you," declares the LORD,
"plans to prosper you and not to harm you, plans to give you
hope and a future."*

—Jeremiah 29:11

15

Diggin' Deeper

Therefore encourage one another and build each other up, just as in fact you are doing.

—1 Thessalonians 5:11

Want more information on the ministries that helped contribute to this book? While neither Youth Specialties nor the author can take responsibility for your interactions with them or what they may or may not provide, you may want to check out their Web sites or send letters via snail mail.

Abstinence

W.A.I.T. (Why Am I Tempted?)

Training in abstinence curriculum toward certification to teach in ministries as well as in high schools

Choosing the Best
2470 Windy Hill Road, Suite 300
Marietta, GA 30067
www.choosingthebest.org

WAITT (Wanting an Individual to Trust)
Biblically based abstinence program
P.O. Box 133
Elm Grove, WI 53122-0133
262/780-0480
www.waitt.org

Camps for Urban Kids

Kids Across America
I'm Third Foundation
1429 Lakeshore Drive
Branson, MO 65616

Peak 3 Outfitters
Equipping mentors with outdoor experiences
20 E. Mount View Lane
Colorado Springs, CO 80907
719/574-6585
www.peak3.org

Cool T-Shirts You Can Customize for Your Group

Church Art Works
890 Promontory Place SE
Salem, OR 97302-1716
877/ONEWAYOUT
www.ChurchArtWorks.com

Dealing with Juvenile Offenders

Straight Ahead Ministries, Inc.

Transforming the lives of juvenile offenders with the message of
Jesus Christ

P.O. Box 1011
Westboro, MA 01581-6011
508/616-9286
www.straightahead.org

Tutoring and Spiritual Growth

Brothas & Sistas United

Tutoring, mentoring, spiritual instruction, and more

Jesus People USA
920 W. Wilson
Chicago, IL 60640
www.jpusa.org

Harambee Christian Family Center

Offers faith-based after-school and summer enrichment programs

1581 Navarro Avenue
Pasadena, CA 91103
626/791-7439
www.harambee.org

Park Avenue Foundation

Equips youth and families for excellence in learning and living

3400 Park Avenue S
Minneapolis, MN 55407
612/822-3755

Hope Unlimited

Offers tutoring and mentoring programs

483 S. Kirkwood
Suite 108
Kirkwood, MO 63122
314/739-9819

More Parachurch Organizations with Cool Mentoring Programs

SLAM! Ministries/Sunshine Gospel Ministries

After-school programming, sports, Bible studies

P.O. Box10615
Chicago, IL 60610

Inner City Impact

After-school programming, Bible studies

2704 West North Avenue
Chicago, IL 60647
800/342-2489
www.icichicago.org

The Other Way Community Center

After-school programming, Bible studies

710 West Fulton
Grand Rapids, MI 49504

S.T.E.P. foundation
Tutoring and other programs for urban teens, including dance
P.O. Box 241347
Montgomery, AL 36124
E-mail: step_mgm@bellsouth.net

Urban Impact
P.O. Box 50223
New Orleans, LA 70150-0223

911 Urban Ministries
3827 W. Ogden Avenue
Chicago, IL 60623

International Efforts

Pathfinders International
Empowering indigenous leaders of the church and ministries
throughout the world
3708 Geneva Place
McHenry, IL 60050

Urban Entrepreneurs

UrbanPromise Ministries
Tutoring, after-school programming, and a cool greeting card business
3700 Rudderow Avenue
Camden, NJ 08105
856/661-1700
www.urbanpromiseusa.org

Work Camp Experiences

The Pittsburgh Project
2801 North Charles Street
Pittsburgh, PA 15214-3110
412/321-1678
www.pittsburghproject.org

Youth Unlimited
Sponsors Project Bridge, where teens from all ethnic backgrounds
work together
P.O. Box 7259
Grand Rapids, MI 49510-7259
(616) 241-5616 ext. 3042
www.gospelcom.net/yu/

When the Street Is Your Church

Emmaus Ministries
Reaches male streetwalkers and prostitutes in Chicago
921 W. Wilson Avenue
Chicago, IL 60640
773/334-6063
www.streets.org

GoodWorks, Inc.

Empowering and transforming lives by providing shelter for the recovering homeless

P.O. Box 4

Athens, OH 45701-0004

740/594-3333

www.good-works.net

Urban Ministry (general)

Christian Community Development Association

A good resource for those involved in any aspect of urban ministry

3827 W. Ogden Avenue

Chicago, IL 60623

773/762-0994

www.ccda.org

Youth Ministry (general)

Youth Specialties

A good resource for those involved in any aspect of youth ministry

300 S. Pierce St.

El Cajon, CA 92020

619/440-2333

www.YouthSpecialties.com

...or you can always bug the author—

Ginger Sinsabaugh

www.TastyFaith.com

About the Author

If Ginger Sinsabaugh can survive urban youth ministry, anyone can. Not letting her small-town roots stop her, Ginger got involved in urban ministry in the early '80s when she moved to Chicago for a job in advertising. While writing jingles paid the rent, Ginger found working with inner-city teens was where her heart really was. So in 1996, she put her advertising career on hold to devote more time to urban youth ministry. Currently Ginger works with SLAM! (Saving Lives in Athletic Ministries), which works hand in hand with Moody Bible Institute to reach teens in Chicago's Cabrini Green projects as well as other high-risk neighborhoods. Ginger and her husband, Jeff, live near Chicago's Wrigley Field.

Resources from Youth Specialties

Youth Ministry Programming

Camps, Retreats, Missions, & Service Ideas (Ideas Library)

Creative Bible Lessons from the Old Testament

Creative Bible Lessons in 1 & 2 Corinthians

Creative Bible Lessons in Galatians and Philippians

Creative Bible Lessons in John: Encounters with Jesus

Creative Bible Lessons in Romans: Faith on Fire!

Creative Bible Lessons on the Life of Christ

Creative Bible Lessons in Psalms

Creative Junior High Programs from A to Z, Vol. 1 (A-M)

Creative Junior High Programs from A to Z, Vol. 2 (N-Z)

Creative Meetings, Bible Lessons, & Worship Ideas (Ideas Library)

Crowd Breakers & Mixers (Ideas Library)

Downloading the Bible Leader's Guide

Drama, Skits, & Sketches (Ideas Library)

Drama, Skits, & Sketches 2 (Ideas Library)

Drama, Skits, & Sketches 3 (Ideas Library)

Dramatic Pauses

Everyday Object Lessons

Games (Ideas Library)

Games 2 (Ideas Library)

Games 3 (Ideas Library)

Good Sex: A Whole-Person Approach to Teenage Sexuality & God

Great Fundraising Ideas for Youth Groups

More Great Fundraising Ideas for Youth Groups

Great Retreats for Youth Groups

Great Talk Outlines for Youth Ministry

Holiday Ideas (Ideas Library)

Hot Illustrations for Youth Talks

More Hot Illustrations for Youth Talks

Still More Hot Illustrations for Youth Talks

Hot Illustrations for Youth Talks 4

Hot Illustrations CD-ROM

Ideas Library on CD-ROM

Incredible Questionnaires for Youth Ministry

Junior High Game Nights

More Junior High Game Nights

Kickstarters: 101 Ingenious Intros to Just about Any Bible Lesson

Live the Life! Student Evangelism Training Kit

Memory Makers

The Next Level Leader's Guide

Play It! Over 150 Great Games for Youth Groups

Roaring Lambs

Screen Play

So What Am I Gonna Do With My Life?

Special Events (Ideas Library)

Spontaneous Melodramas

Spontaneous Melodramas 2

Student Leadership Training Manual

Student Underground: An Event Curriculum on the Persecuted Church

Super Sketches for Youth Ministry

Talking the Walk

Teaching the Bible Creatively

Videos That Teach

What Would Jesus Do? Youth Leader's Kit

Wild Truth Bible Lessons

Wild Truth Bible Lessons 2

Wild Truth Bible Lessons—Pictures of God

Worship Services for Youth Groups

Professional Resources

Administration, Publicity, & Fundraising (Ideas Library)

Dynamic Communicators Workshop

Great Talk Outlines for Youth Ministry

Help! I'm a Junior High Youth Worker!

Help! I'm a Small-Group Leader!

Help! I'm a Sunday School Teacher!

Help! I'm an Urban Youth Worker!

Help! I'm a Volunteer Youth Worker!

How to Expand Your Youth Ministry

How to Speak to Youth...and Keep Them Awake at the Same Time

Junior High Ministry (Updated & Expanded)

The Ministry of Nurture: A Youth Worker's Guide to Discipling Teenagers

Postmodern Youth Ministry

Purpose-Driven® Youth Ministry

Purpose-Driven® Youth Ministry Training Kit

So That's Why I Keep Doing This! 52 Devotional Stories for Youth Workers

A Youth Ministry Crash Course

Youth Ministry Management Tools

The Youth Worker's Handbook to Family Ministry

Academic Resources

Four Views of Youth Ministry & the Church
Starting Right: Thinking Theologically
About Youth Ministry
Youth Ministry That Transforms

Discussion Starters

Discussion & Lesson Starters (Ideas Library)
Discussion & Lesson Starters 2 (Ideas
Library)
EdgeTV
Get 'Em Talking
Keep 'Em Talking!
Good Sex: A Whole-Person Approach to
Teenage Sexuality & God
High School TalkSheets—Updated!
More High School TalkSheets—Updated!
High School TalkSheets from Psalms and
Proverbs—Updated!
Junior High-Middle School
TalkSheets—Updated!
More Junior High-Middle School
TalkSheets—Updated!
Junior High-Middle School TalkSheets from
Psalms and Proverbs—Updated!
Real Kids: Short Cuts
Real Kids: The Real Deal—on Friendship,
Loneliness, Racism, & Suicide
Real Kids: The Real Deal—on Sexual
Choices, Family Matters, & Loss
Real Kids: The Real Deal—on Stressing
Out, Addictive Behavior, Great
Comebacks, & Violence
Real Kids: Word on the Street
Unfinished Sentences: 450 Tantalizing
Statement-Starters to Get Teenagers
Talking & Thinking
What If...? 450 Thought-Provoking
Questions to Get Teenagers Talking,
Laughing, and Thinking
Would You Rather...? 465 Provocative
Questions to Get Teenagers Talking
Have You Ever...? 450 Intriguing Questions
Guaranteed to Get Teenagers Talking

Art Source Clip Art

Youth Group Activities (print)
Clip Art Library Version 2.0 (CD-ROM)

Digital Resources

Clip Art Library Version 2.0 (CD-ROM)
Great Talk Outlines for Youth Ministry
Hot Illustrations CD-ROM
Ideas Library on CD-ROM
Screen Play
Youth Ministry Management Tools

Videos & Video Curricula

Dynamic Communicators Workshop
EdgeTV
Live the Life! Student Evangelism Training
Kit
Purpose-Driven® Youth Ministry Training Kit
Real Kids: Short Cuts
Real Kids: The Real Deal—on Friendship,
Loneliness, Racism, & Suicide
Real Kids: The Real Deal—on Sexual Choices,
Family Matters, & Loss
Real Kids: The Real Deal—on Stressing Out,
Addictive Behavior, Great Comebacks, &
Violence
Real Kids: Word on the Street
Student Underground: An Event Curriculum
on the Persecuted Church
Understanding Your Teenager Video
Curriculum
Youth Ministry Outside the Lines

Student Resources

Downloading the Bible: A Rough Guide to the
New Testament
Downloading the Bible: A Rough Guide to the
Old Testament
Grow For It Journal through the Scriptures
So What Am I Gonna Do With My Life?
Spiritual Challenge Journal: The Next Level
Teen Devotional Bible
What (Almost) Nobody Will Tell You about
Sex
What Would Jesus Do? Spiritual Challenge
Journal
Wild Truth Journal for Junior Highers
Wild Truth Journal—Pictures of God
Wild Truth Journal—Pictures of God 2